THE NORTON LIBRARY

Second Treatise of G

A. JOHN SIMMONS retired ~~as~~ ~~the~~ Hollings-
worth Professor of Philosop~~hy~~ ~~and Law~~ at the Uni-
versity of Virginia, where he h~~ad taught since~~ 1976. He has been
an editor of the journal *Philosop~~hy and Publ~~ic Affairs* since 1982. He
is the author of *Moral Principles and Political Obligations* (Princeton, 1979), *The Lockean Theory of Rights* (Princeton, 1992), *On the
Edge of Anarchy: Locke, Consent, and the Limits of Society* (Princeton, 1993), *Justification and Legitimacy: Essays on Rights and Obligations* (Cambridge, 2000), *Is There a Duty to Obey the Law? For
and Against* (with C. H. Wellman) (Cambridge, 2005), *Political
Philosophy* (Oxford, 2008), and *Boundaries of Authority* (Oxford,
2016), and he has edited the books *International Ethics* (Princeton,
1985) and *Punishment* (Princeton, 1995).

THE NORTON LIBRARY

2021–2022

Euripides, Medea
  Translated by Sheila Murnaghan

Sophocles, Oedipus Tyrannos
  Translated by Emily Wilson

Aristophanes, Lysistrata
  Translated by Aaron Poochigian

Murasaki, The Tale of Genji
  Translated and Abridged by Dennis Washburn

Locke, Second Treatise of Government
  Edited by A. John Simmons

Rousseau, Discourse on the Origin of Inequality
  Translated by Julia Conaway Bondanella and Edited by Frederick Neuhouser

Shelley, Frankenstein
  Edited by Michael Bérubé

Mill, Utilitarianism
  Edited by Peter Singer and Katarzyna de Lazari-Radek

Dostoevsky, Notes from Underground
  Translated by Michael R. Katz

Woolf, Mrs. Dalloway
  Edited by Merve Emre

For a complete list of titles in the Norton Library, visit
wwnorton.com/norton-library

THE NORTON LIBRARY

John Locke
Second Treatise of Government

Edited by

A. John Simmons

W. W. NORTON & COMPANY
Independent Publishers Since 1923

W. W. Norton & Company has been independent since its founding in 1923, when William Warder Norton and Mary D. Herter Norton first published lectures delivered at the People's Institute, the adult education division of New York City's Cooper Union. The firm soon expanded its program beyond the Institute, publishing books by celebrated academics from America and abroad. By midcentury, the two major pillars of Norton's publishing program—trade books and college texts—were firmly established. In the 1950s, the Norton family transferred control of the company to its employees, and today—with a staff of five hundred and hundreds of trade, college, and professional titles published each year—W. W. Norton & Company stands as the largest and oldest publishing house owned wholly by its employees.

Editor: Pete Simon
Associate Editor: Katie Pak
Project Editor: Maura Gaughan
Manufacturing by: LSC Communications
Compositor: Westchester Publishing Services
Book design by: Marisa Nakasone
Production Manager: Jeremy Burton

Library of Congress Cataloging-in-Publication Data

Names: Locke, John, 1632–1704, author. | Simmons, A. John (Alan John),
    1950– editor.
Title: Second treatise of government / John Locke ; edited by A. John Simmons.
Other titles: Essay concerning the true original extent and end of civil government
Description: First edition. | New York : W. W. Norton & Company, 2021. |
    Series: The Norton library | Includes bibliographical references.
Identifiers: LCCN 2020056285 | ISBN 9780393428926 (paperback) |
    ISBN 9780393885101 (epub)
Subjects: LCSH: Political science—Early works to 1800. | Toleration—Early
    works to 1800. | Liberty—Early works to 1800.
Classification: LCC JC153 .L85 2021 | DDC 320.1—dc23
LC record available at https://lccn.loc.gov/2020056285

ISBN: 978-0-393-42892-6 (pbk.)

W. W. Norton & Company, Inc., 500 Fifth Avenue, New York, N.Y. 10110
www.wwnorton.com

W. W. Norton & Company Ltd., 15 Carlisle Street, London W1D 3BS

1 2 3 4 5 6 7 8 9 0

Contents

Introduction

John Locke was born in Somerset in 1632 and lived through a period of extraordinary change and chaos in English political and religious life. The English Civil War—actually a series of three civil wars running from 1642 to 1651—was the backdrop for Locke's youth, pitting Kings Charles I and II's insistence on traditional, largely unlimited monarchical authority over England's political and religious life against Parliament's demands for a more balanced and shared governance of church and state. The victory of Parliamentarian forces in this conflict led ultimately to the 1649 execution of Charles I and to Charles II's 1651 flight into exile in France. During Locke's twenties, England's political structure evolved rapidly, as Locke lived first in the Commonwealth, England no longer being a "kingdom," and then under Oliver Cromwell's Protectorate, and then again under the "restored" Stuart monarchy when Charles II returned from exile to assume the throne in 1660. Through all of these changes Locke's engagement was principally intellectual and academic. He did not become deeply involved in practical political affairs until his forties, during the latter portion of Charles II's reign, when in 1679 the Whig party coalesced as a group demanding the exclusion of Charles's brother James from the royal succession. James was a proponent of absolute monarchy, a Roman Catholic, and a friend to Catholic France, and many feared his rule would end traditional freedoms and subject England to the dominance of foreign powers. Despite powerful opposition and much secret plotting, James II succeeded in becoming king on the death of his brother Charles II in 1685. These developments, along with Locke's new Whig connections, helped to spur not only Locke's politically explosive philosophical writings—writings that offered principled arguments against the path taken by the Stuart monarchs—but as well his likely practical assistance to those planning assassination and rebellion.

Locke was the son of a lawyer and small landowner who served as a captain in the Parliamentary army during the early part of the Civil War. Through the influence of his father's military commander, Locke received an excellent education of the sort generally reserved for the more privileged, concluding at Christ Church, Oxford—where Locke arrived at the age of twenty and with which Locke remained associated in various capacities until 1684 (when he was expelled from the college for his politics, under pressure from the king). Despite his family's Parliamentarian leanings, Locke's early education apparently swung his sympathies in a more traditional direction, and he reportedly welcomed the restoration of the monarchy. Locke's earliest political writings were in fact far more sympathetic to unchecked sovereign authority than readers of his mature work might expect. His gradual conversion to an advocacy of limited government, the political orientation we now associate with Locke, owed much to Locke's relationship with Lord Ashley (later the first Earl of Shaftesbury and Lord Chancellor), in whose London household Locke lived beginning in 1667, serving as Ashley's personal physician and secretary and tutor to Ashley's son and grandson, while also occupying some minor political positions.

Locke's relationship to Shaftesbury also eventually placed him in considerable personal danger. Shaftesbury was one of the founders and principal leaders of the Whig movement; he played a central role in the effort to exclude a Catholic monarch, was charged with treason, twice spent time imprisoned in the Tower, plotted rebellion, and ultimately had to flee England for Holland. Locke himself was likely involved in an assassination plot against King Charles II and his brother James, but his writings during this period would alone have been sufficient to subject him to charges of treason. His *Two Treatises of Government* were probably largely completed during the very early 1680s (possibly at Shaftesbury's request), at a time when others were being imprisoned and executed for thinking and writing what Locke thought and wrote. Locke concealed his authorship of the *Treatises*—and of *A Letter Concerning Toleration*, in which Locke argues for a separation of church and state—throughout the remainder of his life.

The *Second Treatise of Government*, while not the first such defense, was certainly this period's most philosophically sophisticated defense of Whig and broadly liberal principles of political philosophy; and the *Second Treatise*'s arguments for natural equality, limited government by consent, and a right of resistance constituted not just an attack on the newly influential theoretical rejections of such ideas, but a direct attack on the crown itself. Even after Locke followed Shaftesbury into exile in Holland to avoid arrest in England, he lived in hiding under an assumed name and was spied on and followed by

English agents. He was eventually named by the English government as a wanted conspirator in connection with the disastrously unsuccessful 1685 effort by the Duke of Monmouth (Charles II's oldest illegitimate son) to overthrow and replace the new King James. The subsequent collapse of James II's rule in the "Glorious" or "Bloodless" Revolution (which was effectively an internal coup d'etat in which the anti-Catholic William of Orange was invited to invade England), along with the Convention Parliament's offer of the throne to William and Mary, brought Locke back to England in 1689, after five years in Holland, as a respected supporter of the new regime and as the soon-to-be-famous author of *An Essay Concerning Human Understanding*. Even in this new, far safer climate, however, where Locke rapidly became a very influential and even revered figure, he published his *Two Treatises of Government* anonymously and only acknowledged his authorship in his will, after his death in 1704—perhaps because Locke feared a return by James, perhaps because he knew that his popular-consent-based justification for William's authority in fact contradicted the new king's own, more traditional (i.e., hereditary) view of it. Locke spent the final years of his life residing in the home of his longtime friend Lady Masham, daughter of the philosopher Ralph Cudworth.

Rights and Duties in the *Second Treatise*

Locke's *Second Treatise of Government* occupies a remarkable place in intellectual history: it was enormously influential both in its own and later practical political contexts and as a great theoretical work in political philosophy. It was written during a time of political crisis, when it was sometimes used to justify a course of political resistance or rebellion. Later, it more prominently served as a cornerstone of revolutionary thought in America and France.

But the *Second Treatise* is also sufficiently rich in ideas and arguments to have captured the philosophical imaginations of thinkers as diverse as the young Karl Marx and the Harvard libertarian philosopher Robert Nozick. While described by Locke only as "an essay concerning the true original extent and end of civil government," the *Second Treatise* in fact insightfully discusses a wide range of topics, such as the source of private property, the morality of punishment and reparation, morality in marriage and the family, rights and duties in war, self-defense, slavery and servitude, conquest, tyranny, and revolution.

Much sophisticated work has been devoted to dating, identifying, and describing the historical and political context of the *Second Treatise*, and I will not try to summarize or add to that work here. For whatever practical roles Locke's work played during his own and later tumultuous times, the *Second Treatise* is still first and foremost a work of philosophy. Locke's arguments and conclusions are designed not simply to mesh with and rationalize his Whig political sympathies, but to address the great theoretical questions about rights, property, and governmental legitimacy raised by earlier political philosophers. While philosophy may not have been Locke's first academic love (he was initially more interested in science and medicine), and while he may have become in some sense a revolutionary, from his first substantial writings at Oxford—on morality, religion, and politics—Locke was writing as a philosopher, concerned with complex questions of theory and aiming to satisfy (as he asserts in his epitaph) "the demands solely of truth." I will concentrate here on some of the philosophical content of the book.

The *Second Treatise of Government* is, of course, a book about the moral foundations of government. But in service to that inquiry, it explores far more widely the natures and sources of all our moral rights and duties; and as we will see, the book is organized accordingly.

While Locke uses various synonyms for both moral rights (e.g., powers, privileges, claims, liberties) and duties (e.g., bonds, obligations), his arguments make it clear that it is moral rights and duties he is discussing. Locke concentrates on the various kinds of human relationships that give rise to moral rights and duties, and on the ways in which the natures of those relationships shape and limit the rights and duties they define. Some rights and duties, for instance, are a simple function of our relationship with God—he as creator and we as his creatures—and some arise from our relationships with our parents or children. Some rights we have because people have wronged us or others. Locke also discusses a wide range of rights and duties that arise from the voluntary relationships into which we can choose or choose not to enter—for example, property rights over the parts of unowned nature on which we decide to labor, masters' rights over those we choose to employ as servants, conjugal rights with respect to our chosen spouses, and economic rights arising from our contracts with others.

For Locke's specific purposes in the *Second Treatise*, the most important of these voluntarily acquired rights and duties are, of course, the moral rights and duties that Locke believes arise from popular political consent. In this treatise *of government*, of course, the final aim of Locke's theorizing is to explicate the rights and duties of citizens on the one hand, and of rulers or governments on the other. The book probably began as an attempt to justify the exclusion of the Catholic James from the English throne, but it ended as an attempt to "make good" the new King William's "title in the consent of the people," as he puts it in his Preface. Locke tries to explain a king's, or *magistrate*'s, "right to rule" in the *Second Treatise* by contrasting the source and nature of political rights and duties with the source and nature of rights and duties arising from other kinds of relationships discussed in the book. In Locke's view, political rights and duties had frequently been confused with or wrongly subsumed under the rights and duties that arise from three other sources: from our relationship with God, with rulers enjoying divine rights over subjects and subjects with a duty to obey the powers that be; from our relationship with our parents, with rulers possessing paternal power over subjects and subjects bound by filial duties; and from our relationship with those who wield coercive physical power over us, including not only conquerors, but also our local political rulers, with might making right. But rightful political power (i.e., genuine *authority*), Locke argues in the *Second Treatise*, is neither divine (ordained by God), paternal (identical to or like that of our parents), nor despotical (the result of subjugation or conquest or enslavement) (§169).

Political Authority and the State of Nature

Consider how the *Second Treatise* is structured. In chapter 1, §2, Locke identifies his task as that of clarifying how he understands "political power" in order to distinguish it from other kinds of "powers" with which it might be confused. By "power" here, Locke means moral right—that is, he means rightful or legitimate authority, not physical power—since he goes on to define political power (in §3) as "a *right* of making laws." To help make clear the differences between political power and other kinds of powers, Locke then introduces the idea of the state of nature in chapter 2. State-of-nature stories are not unusual in political philosophy, of course, especially among those who employ the idea of a social contract, but Locke's version has some striking features. His account of life without government and law, while far less grim and pessimistic than that of, say, Thomas Hobbes, nonetheless does follow the by now familiar line: the threat of conflict and possible war would give people in a stateless condition very good reason to create a civil government (e.g., §123). Locke importantly departs from Hobbes, however. He does so first in imagining the possibility of real cooperation in the state of nature: not only in people living together in communities, entering into contracts, trading goods, and inventing money, but also in assisting one another in the prelegal enforcement of their natural rights. Even though it does make sense to try to improve our lot in such a condition by creating a more secure civil society, Locke argues, it cannot be true that just any kind of political society, no matter how awful, would be rationally preferable to our natural condition so described (§93). Second, Locke, unlike Hobbes, argues that a set of familiar moral duties and rights bind all of us, as much in the state of nature as out of it (where for Hobbes, there is no right or wrong, just or unjust, in the state of nature/war).

The natural condition of people, Locke claims, is "a *state of perfect freedom* to order their actions and dispose of their possessions and persons, as they think fit." It is also a condition "of *equality*, wherein all the power and jurisdiction is reciprocal, no one having more than another" (§4). Locke later clarifies that the equality he has in mind is not equality in all things, but only in persons' "*equal right* to . . . *natural freedom*"—that is, in our equal right not to be "subjected to the will or authority of any other man" without our consent (§54). The condition of "natural freedom" is also not as "perfect" as these initial remarks suggest. For "the *state of nature* has a law of nature to govern it," which requires not only that we not "harm another in his life, health, liberty, or possessions," but that we likewise preserve ourselves (§6). This is God's law for his creatures, the law of reason, "an eternal rule to all men" (§135). We have the moral right to dispose of our "possessions and persons" in a state of nature, but only where we can do so without harming self or others. What, then, of those who choose to disregard this law of nature? "In transgressing the law of nature," Locke argues, "the offender declares himself to live by another rule than that of reason and common equity . . . and so he becomes dangerous to mankind" (§8).

Locke argues that persons all naturally possess an "executive right"—a right to punish a wrongdoer, with or without the help of others, in order to "retribute to him, so far as calm reason and conscience dictate, what is proportionate to his transgression" (§8). Locke acknowledges that such universal vigilantism is likely to lead to conflict in a state of nature—due to the influence of partiality, passion, and the desire for revenge on our judgments—and he argues that "civil government is the proper remedy" for such conflict (§§13, 21). Indeed, a distinctive feature of Locke's account is that he plainly regards the primary difference between the state of nature and "civil" (i.e., rightful or legitimate) society as turning on this natural executive right: only where everyone has surrendered their natural right to punish—allowing a neutral, impartial judge, or *umpire* (§87), to do the job of punishing wrongdoers for them—do we have a real, civil society. The legitimate presence of "a known and indifferent judge" (§125) is the chief mark of civil society (§89), and its absence marks the state of nature (§§19, 87, 89). The "judge" is the government that the members of society choose to create (§132), which, having collected the individual executive rights surrendered by that society's members, exercises that society's executive power for them.

It may seem that Locke's beginning chapter 2 with this account of our natural condition (i.e., by explicitly contrasting it with the condition of civil society) simply assumes what he is trying to show—namely, that political authority and subjection are *not* part of our natural condition. After all, we can hardly be free and equal by nature if we are by nature subject to the political authority of some ruler whose superiority can limit our freedom and equality with laws or commands. The complaint would be fair, of course, if the book ended with chapter 2. But Locke is here simply stating the position he'll argue for in the remainder of the book. He has already argued against Sir Robert Filmer in the *First Treatise* (as he says in §1 of the *Second*) that we cannot be naturally subject to our rulers in virtue of God's "positive donation" of authority to Adam, authority handed down and finally inherited by contemporary monarchs. And he plausibly assumes (in §4) that there has been no "manifest declaration" of God's will that imbues any contemporary monarch(s) with divine authority over us. It only remains for Locke to show that *other* possible "natural" justifications for political authority *fail*.

He shows this by arguing, first (in chapters 2–4), that perhaps the most apparent "natural" fact about us—that we are nearly all born into governed societies, subject to the state's threat of irresistible political coercion—cannot suffice to show that our political superiors naturally hold rightful or legitimate political power over us. Some uses of coercion, of course, are permissible and some are not. We know Locke's view: natural law prohibits our harming others (including limiting their liberty and taking their possessions) "unless it be to do justice on an offender" (§6). So the only permissible use of force against others must be a proportionate response to others' wrongdoing. Unjust or wrongful coercion makes the wrongdoer vulnerable to punishment by whomever cares to exercise their executive rights. Wrongdoing diminishes the wrongdoer's rights, rendering morally permissible treatment of him that would, in the absence of that wrong, count as unjust harm. Locke sometimes uses the idea of *forfeiture* of rights—nonvoluntary loss of rights because of wrongdoing—to explain this diminishment of a wrongdoer's rights (e.g., in §§23, 172–73), in the same way that we sometimes now say that criminals have forfeited certain of their legal rights (e.g., to liberty). Since we are not wrongdoers at birth, Locke draws one obvious conclusion from this reasoning: the mere fact that we are born under governments cannot justify or render rightful governments' claims of authority over us or their subjecting us from birth to political coercion. Thus, Locke later (in chapter 8) concludes that there is no force to claims "that *by being born under any government, we are naturally subjects to it*" (§116).

The most dramatic case of forfeiture of rights discussed by Locke takes place when one person makes war on another—when a person declares "by word or action" the intention to take away another's life or freedom (§§16–17). Such warmaking results in the forfeiture of *all* rights, reducing the warmaker to the moral status of a dangerous, wild beast who is "not capable of any property" (§85)—i.e., of any moral rights. Warmakers may be killed by any person, as a proportionate response warranted by that person's executive right. Interestingly, warmakers may also be justly enslaved (§23), just slavery being "nothing else but *the state of war continued between a lawful conqueror and a captive*" (§24). This, for Locke, is the only possible instance of morally justified slavery; he has rejected all the other familiar philosophical attempts to justify its practice. Against the (Aristotelian) doctrine of "slaves by nature," Locke has argued that all persons are by nature free and equal. Against Filmer's argument that parents own their children, and so have absolute power over them, we will see that Locke counters with a detailed defense of the limited and short-term nature of parental rights over children. And where philosophers like Grotius and Hobbes take seriously the possibility that persons could *make* themselves slaves by freely compacting with their lords, Locke specifically argues that, having been given by God's law no right to kill oneself, one "*cannot*, by compact or his own consent, *enslave himself,*" giving another the arbitrary power "to take away his life when he pleases" (§§23, 135, 168). Finally, as we have seen, Locke counters the view that simple conquest or wielding irresistible physical power over another can give one absolute dominion over him (a position defended by Hobbes and many others, and dealt with at length by Locke in chapter 16). Locke holds that, far from giving the conqueror new rights over others, unjust conquest instead results in the forfeiture of most or of all the rights of the conqueror—thus justifying resistance and punishment by the unjustly conquered (§176).

Only in the case of captives taken in a *just* war (that is, in a war undertaken to defend, or to seek restitution for the violation of, our most basic rights to life and freedom) is despotical power over another—the absolute authority of a lord over a slave—morally rightful (§172). Locke's arguments against absolute *government* then proceed in precisely the same fashion as his arguments against slavery, but in this case without the "just war" exception. Absolute or arbitrary government—that is, unlimited sovereign authority that permits rulers to rightfully do or command anything at all—is for Locke a simple moral impossibility, since it in effect amounts to political slavery (with each subject being a "slave, of an absolute prince" [§91]). As with slavery, our natural freedom and equality preclude arguments that the absolute authority of monarchs is natural; monarchs cannot rule absolutely under the guise of parents, and we cannot even voluntarily create absolute authority for monarchs by our consent or compacts. What then of the political analogue of Locke's single instance of justified slavery? What of the case of a just conqueror who rules over a conquered nation that had unjustly made war against him? Locke responds that even if just conquerors have despotical power over those who warred against them, other, innocent residents of that nation cannot justly be ruled despotically, nor can the conqueror seize the warmaker's goods (to which the warmaker's wife and children have superior claims [§§178–79, 183]) or the nation's land. There can be no such thing as legitimate despotical *political* authority that reaches all of a nation's residents and involves exercising jurisdiction over all of its property; there can only be mass enslavement of captured warmakers (§189). Thus, Locke can conclude that "*absolute monarchy*, which by some men is counted the only government in the world, is indeed *inconsistent with civil society* and so can be no form of civil government at all" (§90).

Consent, Limited Government, and Resistance

The next stage of Locke's argument against "natural" justifications for political authority comes in chapter 6, where he maintains that the other obvious "natural" fact about us—namely, that we all have parents—could not justify *their* wielding political authority over us, nor could it justify kings doing so as "fathers of their countries." Not only do mothers have equal claim with fathers to parental authority—so that contemporary kings could hardly claim *sole* political authority on these grounds (§52–53)—but parental authority is too limited in both scope and duration to constitute or even resemble political authority. Parental government is "natural," but not "political" (§170). Indeed, parental authority is only a "temporary government" (§67) and includes only that power which is necessary to discharge parental *duties* to "take care of their offspring during the imperfect state of childhood" (§58). As Locke much later concludes, parental ("paternal") power is only "for the benefit of their

children during their minority" (§173). While it was perhaps "natural" in "the first ages of the world" for "the
father of the family to become the prince of it," such
political subjection to the father was never the *natural*
condition of the children (§§105–7). It was "the express
or tacit consent of the children when they were grown
up" that gave their father political authority over them
(§74).

If political authority is not *natural*—if "all the power
and jurisdiction is reciprocal" in our natural condition,
and political authority must be "artificial" (i.e., created
by persons' actions)—then, Locke reasons, there remains
only one possible source of political authority and subjection that takes seriously the moral rights we naturally
possess. If we are "by nature all free, equal, and independent," the only foundation for political authority that
respects this natural freedom—that is, the only way that
political authority can arise legitimately, without wrong-
ing us—is our own freely given *consent*. Political subjection that is freely accepted can be rightful or legitimate,
provided only that we do not consent to more than we
have a right to allow (such as political slavery, the absolute dominion of a monarch). Our consent, unlike our
wrongdoing, *can* justify *political* coercion—the law-
governed restraint and requirements administered by a
freely created government. Thus, Locke's conclusion: "no
one can be put out of this estate [i.e., the state of nature]
and subjected to the political power of another without
his own consent" (§95).

This, of course, is Locke's famous "consent theory"
of political authority and obligation, which did much to
inspire Jefferson's Declaration and the views of other
American founders. People can consent together to create a new civil society, or individuals can consent to the
terms of incorporation of existing legitimate societies in
order to join them (§89). But in all cases, rightful political

power must be exercised within the terms of popular consent; and in no cases can it be absolute, since we lack the right to give another "arbitrary power" over our lives (§23). The consent that binds people to obey their rightful authorities must be given freely (*"promises extorted by force . . . bind not at all"* [§186]), but it can be given either expressly, as in an explicit oath of allegiance, or tacitly. Locke, however, notoriously asserts that tacit consent to a government's authority is given even by "the very being of any one within the territories of that government" (§119), a consent of which "people take no notice" (§117). Locke here threatens to undercut the very rationale for appealing to consent as the sole basis of rightful author-ity in the first place—namely, that deliberate free choice of political allegiance is compatible with our natural freedom.

Understood in the context of Locke's consent theory, it is now somewhat easier to see what he means (and does not mean) by "the state of nature." The state-of-nature story that Locke tells in chapters 2 and 3 might initially seem, despite the differences noted above, to show at least that Locke's *concept* of the state of nature is more or less the same as Hobbes's. Both tell a story about government being necessary in order to avoid war and other "incon-veniencies," as Locke calls them (§§13, 136, listing them more fully in §§124–26). For Hobbes, remember, the state of nature was simply any "ungoverned" condition of per-sons, any condition in which people live together without a powerful sovereign (government, law) ruling over them, one threatening them with harm unless they behave peacefully. Though Hobbes, unlike Locke, might pessi-mistically think of such a condition as a virtual "moral vacuum" in which life is a "solitary, poor, nasty, brutish, and short" condition of "war of all against all," it still might seem that they at least *mean* the same thing by "the state of nature"—namely, an ungoverned condition. That Hobbes and Locke do not define the state of nature the same way can be seen in Locke's conclusion to chapter 2, where he says of the state of nature "that all men are naturally in that state, and remain so, until by their own consents they make themselves members of some politic society" (§15). Similarly, "all princes and rulers of *independent* governments all through the world are in a state of nature" (§14). But, of course, most of us do not live in an ungoverned condition—we are not "in it naturally"—and all princes and rulers live in societies that are governed, albeit by them. So Locke's most prominent remarks about the state of nature indicate that he simply cannot have in mind the same thing being discussed by Hobbes and many other social contract thinkers.

For Locke the state of nature is not a *social* condition of being "ungoverned," as it is for Hobbes. For Locke, the state of nature is a *moral* condition, the condition of not being a consenting member of some legitimate (i.e., consensual) civil society. What "puts an end to the state of nature between men" is their "agreeing together mutually to enter into one community" (§14). Each of us is born into the state of nature and must remain there at least until we reach the "age of consent." Should we consent to membership in a civil society, we then leave the state of nature with respect to our fellow citizens who have also consented to membership in this civil society. But we remain *in* the state of nature with respect to all persons who are not members of our own society (and with respect to fellow subjects should we live in an illegitimate, nonconsensual society [§145]), just as princes and rulers all remain in the state of nature with respect to one another (§184). Indeed, barring the surprising creation of a consensual world-state, each of us remains perpetually in the state of nature with respect to most (and perhaps all) people in the world. This is not to say, with Hobbes, that we are in a state of war with all of these people, bound by no moral duties. Rather, it is just to say that there are certain distinctively political duties that we do not have toward them. We of course may not murder, assault, steal from, or enslave Russians or Italians, despite our being in the state of nature with respect to them. The state of nature, for Locke, is a moral condition that still, but *only*, involves our being obligated (after reaching the age of reason) by the law of nature. However, those *out* of the state of nature with respect to one another—that is, those in civil society with one another—are bound not only by natural law, but also by the mutual political obligations they have consensually undertaken. These new, "artificially" created obligations include the obligations to obey the law and to abide by and assist in enforcing the rulings of an impartial judge—the government and laws. Those within civil society together create these new political obligations by freely agreeing to limit their natural freedom, most importantly by voluntarily surrendering their natural executive rights.

When we understand the logical structure of the *Second Treatise* in the way I've suggested above, and understand the "original of political power" as "mutual consent" (§171), the remaining themes and arguments in the book (concerning the "extent and end of civil government") unfold quite naturally. Locke's discussions of the possible forms of a commonwealth and of the limits on legislative power (in chapters 10 and 11) simply explore the options available to naturally free persons in creating a government for themselves and the limits natural law places on those options. While God has entrusted us with lives to live, according to our own preferences and interests, he has not given us "perfect" freedom to do with ourselves as we please. We may not give away or otherwise do away with our lives or freedom. That restriction on our conduct—along with the necessary conditions for being a civil society at all—restricts as well what we may do in empowering a government over us (e.g., our government may not be absolute, it must rule as an impartial umpire). While Locke does, of course, write in places of persons having "property" in themselves (e.g., §§27, 44), he has earlier made it perfectly clear that we are all ultimately the property of God, who has a creator's absolute rights over us and who places limits on what we may do with "our" property (§§6, 56). And because there are corresponding moral limits on the ways in which we may empower our governments, we cannot understand political power as simply *given* to governments. Rather, governments are only *entrusted* with such power; they are given only the *fiduciary* authority to act for certain ends and within certain limits (§§142, 149). Because governments are thus only *trustees* of the people, not contractual "owners" of the rights that members have surrendered to them, the people retain the right to judge when the terms of that trust have been exceeded and to "discard" their trustee when they so judge (§§149, 168, 240).

The distinctions between the different powers entrusted to governments and the subordination of those powers (the subjects of chapters 12 and 13) also follow from the earlier discussion of the natural origins of those powers. The different powers—to make domestic laws, to enforce them, and to act internationally—simply correspond to the various aspects of "the power every man naturally had before he entered into society" (§145), now surrendered by each member to society. And just as the divine lawgiver must be superior in authority to the creatures he has authorized to enforce his law, so too the legislative power in society must be superior to the executive ("For what can give laws to another must needs be superior to him" [§150]). Locke's closing discussions of usurpation, tyranny, and dissolution of government (in chapters 17, 18, and 19) are similarly designed to lay out the implications of the preceding model of fiduciary government within a voluntary, consensual society. But it is also, of course, impossible to read these chapters of the *Second Treatise* without seeing them as a list of actual charges against Kings Charles and James, all justifying resistance to the crown—indeed, not just resistance by Parliament, or by leaders of the people, or by the people as a whole, but resistance by "any single man" (§168) or "private men" (§208) who are wronged and denied appeal to an impartial judge to decide their cases. Further, Locke repeatedly characterizes these abuses by the crown as initiating a state of war with the people (e.g., §§155, 227, 232), and we have already seen the moral consequences of making war on the innocent. While it may well be fair to respond that not all of the wrongs with which Locke charges the Stuart monarchs of his day really look like "warmaking" efforts to kill or enslave their subjects (and that Locke opportunistically expands the meaning of "state of war" as the book approaches its conclusion), there seems little doubt that Locke intends to defend in the closing chapters of the *Second Treatise* a very radical theory of the right of armed, popular resistance to unjust government. It is thus no surprise that he was not eager for his authorship of the *Second Treatise* to become known.

Private Property

In all of this I have yet to mention the role of chapter 5 of the *Second Treatise*, "Of Property," and that may seem puzzling. For Locke's account of the possibility and source of natural (moral) property rights and of the limits on such rights may well be the most famous and influential chapter in this famous and influential book. Chapter 5, of course, concerns "property" in the narrow sense—that is, rights over external things in the world, or "estate" (as opposed to "property" in the broader sense of any of our rights, including our "lives, liberties, and estates" [§§123, 173]). Locke's solution here to the great natural-law puzzle of the original community of the earth—that that community seems inconsistent with the possibility of private property—did much to undercut the natural-law tradition's "communist" themes for future defenders of "capitalism," even as his labor theory of "use value" perhaps did the opposite. And his well-known labor theory of property acquisition captures one of our most widely shared intuitions about property: namely, that things ought to belong to those who labor to make them. That said, however, it is not immediately evident how the arguments of chapter 5 fit into the overall strategy of the book as I have outlined it above. The chapter appears to be taking up a completely new topic, one that is, even if it concerns our natural moral rights, apparently unconnected to the surrounding text's efforts to explicate the idea of "political power." This fact has long fueled speculation that Locke's chapter on property began as a freestanding essay, with Locke somewhat awkwardly forcing it into an otherwise continuous and thematically unified text.

In response to these concerns, several points seem worth making. First, of course, "harm to possessions" is one of the harms prohibited by God's law, and we cannot understand in what this harm consists without understanding the origin of and limits on natural property rights. Second, the account of property in chapter 5—and of the invention of money, with its legitimation of material inequality (§50)—plainly supports some more general "free-market" economic positions which were important to Locke's view of the best kind of political society. Third, Locke's attempt to explain how private property could justly arise out of the original community of the earth— "and that without any express compact of all the commoners" (§25)—is Locke's contribution to solving one of the central problems of the natural law tradition, and Locke could hardly hope to forge ahead in that tradition without addressing the problem. Last, and perhaps most important for Locke's purposes in the *Two Treatises*, chapter 5 constitutes an important piece in Locke's efforts to completely refute Filmer's arguments in favor of sovereign absolutism. While "Of Property" does not specifically name Filmer as its target, §25 (and, to a certain extent, the rest of the chapter) is plainly intended to counter Filmer's claim that contemporary monarchs can be understood to own their countries in the way that Adam originally owned the earth, and that ordinary individuals could never have come to have private property of their own (without universal consent) that could counter monarchical claims to it. Indeed, the overall argument of chapter 5 continues Locke's important arguments in §§41–43 of the *First Treatise*. There Locke argues that ownership of land cannot give one political power over others: "possession even of the whole earth" cannot "give anyone a sovereign arbitrary authority over the persons of men" (*First Treatise*, §41). Chapter 5 of the *Second Treatise* extends these claims. Humankind's "right to their preservation" (§25) requires that they have as well a right to make sufficient private property in unowned nature to guarantee their independence from those who would use landownership to coercively impose political subjection.

Locke is often referred to as "the father of liberalism." While there is no single view or philosophy that can uncontroversially claim the title "liberalism," it is certainly true that Locke was an early defender of many of the key tenets we associate with modern liberalism— such as individual rights to freedom and equality, limited government, popular sovereignty, private property, and the separation of church and state. And Locke's philosophical attacks on tyranny and absolute government in the *Second Treatise* profoundly influenced thinkers like Rousseau and Jefferson, helping to provide justifications for the eighteenth-century "liberal revolutions" in America and France (and elsewhere).

Locke's political philosophy also continues to serve as a basis for many views in contemporary political philosophy/theory, inspiring theorists on both sides of the contemporary liberal "divide" between liberal egalitarianism and libertarianism. Liberal egalitarians—most prominently John Rawls and his many followers—emphasize the Lockean themes of freedom and equality, advocating for political principles that would be chosen by free and equal persons under genuinely fair conditions of choice. Libertarians have instead emphasized Lockean arguments for minimal government and a free-market economy. Still other contemporary liberals—often referred to as "left-libertarians"—have tried to develop an intermediate position, one that takes seriously both the Lockean liberties stressed by libertarians and the Lockean concern for full and fair equality that helps to guide liberal egalitarianism. The central themes of the *Second Treatise* thus continue to reverberate throughout contemporary theoretical developments of liberalism.

A Note on the Text

The text is based on the version of the *Second Treatise* found in the sixth (1764) edition of Locke's *Two Treatises of Government*, which incorporated all of Locke's personal corrections to earlier editions. I have extensively altered Locke's punctuation in order to eliminate ambiguity and to make the text more readable. Some spelling has been modernized, and some of the wording has been very slightly changed, either where this would help to clarify Locke's meaning or where the sixth edition is inconsistent with all earlier ones. None of these changes should in any way affect the sense, emphases, or "flavor" of Locke's text.

John Locke

Second Treatise of Government

TWO TREATISES OF GOVERNMENT
BY JOHN LOCKE

SALUS POPULI SUPREMA LEX ESTO

LONDON PRINTED MDCLXXXVIIII
REPRINTED, THE SIXTH TIME, BY A. MILLAR, H.
WOODFALL, I. WHISTON AND B. WHITE, I. RI-
VINGTON, L. DAVIS AND C. REYMERS, R. BALD-
WIN, HAWES CLARKE AND COLLINS; W. IOHN-
STON, W. OWEN, I. RICHARDSON, S. CROWDER,
T. LONGMAN, B. LAW, C. RIVINGTON, E.
DILLY, R. WITHY, C. AND R. WARE, S. BAKER,
T. PAYNE, A. SHUCKBURGH, I. HINXMAN
MDCCLXIIII

The present edition of this book has not only been collated with the first three editions, which were published during the author's life, but also has the advantage of his last corrections and improvements, from a copy delivered by him to Mr. Peter Coste, communicated to the Editor, and now lodged in Christ College, Cambridge.

TWO TREATISES OF GOVERNMENT.
IN THE FORMER THE FALSE PRIN-
CIPLES AND FOUNDATION OF SIR
ROBERT FILMER AND HIS FOL-
LOWERS ARE DETECTED AND
OVERTHROWN.
THE LATTER IS AN ESSAY CON-
CERNING THE TRUE ORIGINAL
EXTENT AND END OF CIVIL
GOVERNMENT.

Preface

Reader, thou hast here the beginning and end of a discourse concerning government; what fate has otherwise disposed of the papers that should have filled up the middle, and were more than all the rest, it is not worthwhile to tell thee. These which remain I hope are sufficient to establish the throne of our great restorer, our present King William; to make good his title in the consent of the people, which being the only one of all lawful governments, he has more fully and clearly than any prince in Christendom; and to justify to the world the people of England, whose love of their just and natural rights, with their resolution to preserve them, saved the nation when it was on the very brink of slavery and ruin.° If these papers have that evidence I flatter myself is to be found in them, there will be no great miss of those which are lost, and my reader may be satisfied without them. For I imagine I shall have neither the time nor inclination to repeat my pains and fill up the wanting part of my answer, by tracing Sir Robert again through all the windings and obscurities which are to be met with in the several branches of his wonderful system. The king and body of the nation have since so thoroughly confuted his hypothesis that I suppose nobody hereafter will have either the confidence to appear against our common safety, and be again an advocate for slavery, or the weakness to be deceived with contradictions dressed up in a popular style and well-turned periods. For if anyone will be at the pains himself, in those parts which are here untouched, to strip Sir Robert's discourses of the flourish of doubtful expressions and endeavour to reduce his words to direct, positive, intelligible propositions, and then compare them one with another, he will quickly be satisfied there was never so much glib nonsense put together in well-sounding English. If he think it not worthwhile to examine his works all through, let him make an experiment in that part where he treats of usurpation. And let him try whether he can, with all his skill, make Sir Robert intelligible and consistent with himself or common sense. I should not speak so plainly of a gentleman, long since past answering, had not the pulpit, of late years, publicly owned his doctrine and made it the current divinity of the times. It is necessary those men who, taking on them to be teachers, have so dangerously misled others, should be openly showed of what authority this their Patriarch is whom they have so blindly followed, that so they may either retract what upon so ill grounds they have vented and cannot be maintained, or else justify those principles which they preached up for gospel, though they had no better an author than an English courtier. For I should not have written against Sir Robert, or taken the pains to show his mistakes, inconsistencies, and want of (what he so much boasts of, and pretends wholly to build on) scripture-proofs, were there not men amongst us who, by crying up his books and espousing his doctrine, save me from the reproach of writing against a dead adversary. They have been so zealous in this point that, if I have done him any wrong, I cannot hope they should spare me. I wish where they have done the truth and the public wrong, they would be as ready to redress it and allow its just weight to this reflection, viz. that there cannot be done a greater mischief to prince and people than propagating wrong notions concerning government, that so at last all times might not have reason to complain of the Drum Ecclesiastic. If anyone, concerned really for truth, undertake the confutation of my hypothesis, I promise him either to recant my mistake, upon fair conviction, or to answer his difficulties. But he must remember two things:

First, that caviling here and there at some expression or little incident of my discourse is not an answer to my book.

Secondly, that I shall not take railing for arguments, nor think either of these worth my notice, though I shall always look on myself as bound to give satisfaction to anyone who shall appear to be conscientiously scrupulous in the point and shall show any just grounds for his scruples.

I have nothing more but to advertise the reader that Observations stands for Observations on Hobbs, Milton, &c. and that a bare quotation of pages always means pages of his Patriarcha, Edition 1680.

CHAPTER I

The Introduction†

§. 1. It having been shown in the foregoing discourse,

1. That *Adam* had not, either by natural right of fatherhood or by positive donation from God, any such authority over his children, or dominion over the world, as is pretended.

2. That if he had, his heirs, yet, had no right to it.

3. That if his heirs had, there being no law of nature nor positive law of God that determines which is the right heir in all cases that may arise, the right of succession, and consequently of bearing rule, could not have been certainly determined.

4. That if even that had been determined, yet the knowledge of which is the eldest line of *Adam*'s posterity, being so long since utterly lost that in the races of mankind and families of the world there remains not to one

---

† All footnotes printed here are from the sixth edition (1764) of Locke's *Two Treatises of Government*. For the Editor's notes to this Norton Library edition, see Notes, p. 187.

above another the least pretense to be the eldest house and to have the right of inheritance.

All these premises having, as I think, been clearly made out, it is impossible that the rulers now on earth should make any benefit or derive any the least shadow of authority from that which is held to be the fountain of all power, *Adam's private dominion and paternal jurisdiction;* so that he that will not give just occasion to think that all government in the world is the product only of force and violence, and that men live together by no other rules but that of beasts, where the strongest carries it, and so lay a foundation for perpetual disorder and mischief, tumult, sedition and rebellion (things that the followers of that hypothesis so loudly cry out against), must of necessity find out another rise of government, another original of political power, and another way of designing and knowing the persons that have it, than what Sir *Robert Filmer* hath taught us.°

§. 2. To this purpose, I think it may not be amiss to set down what I take to be political power, that the power of a *magistrate* over a subject may be distinguished from that of a *father* over his children, a *master* over his servant, a *husband* over his wife, and a *lord* over his slave. All which distinct powers happening sometimes together in the same man, if he be considered under these different relations, it may help us to distinguish these powers one from another and show the difference between a ruler of a commonwealth, a father of a family, and a captain of a galley.

§. 3. *Political power,* then, I take to be a *right* of making laws with penalties of death, and consequently all less penalties, for the regulating and preserving of property, and of employing the force of the community in the execution of such laws and in the defence of the commonwealth from foreign injury, and all this only for the public good.

CHAPTER II

Of the State of Nature

§. 4. To understand political power right and derive it from its original, we must consider what state all men are naturally in, and that is a *state of perfect freedom* to order their actions and dispose of their possessions and persons, as they think fit, within the bounds of the law of nature, without asking leave or depending upon the will of any other man.

A *state* also *of equality*, wherein all the power and jurisdiction is reciprocal, no one having more than another; there being nothing more evident than that creatures of the same species and rank, promiscuously born to all the same advantages of nature and the use of the same faculties, should also be equal one amongst another without subordination or subjection, unless the lord and master of them all should, by any manifest declaration of his will, set one above another and confer on him, by an evident and clear appointment, an undoubted right to dominion and sovereignty.

§. 5. This *equality* of men by nature, the judicious *Hooker*°
looks upon as so evident in itself and beyond all question,
that he makes it the foundation of that obligation to
mutual love amongst men on which he builds the duties
they owe one another, and from whence he derives the
great maxims *of justice* and *charity.* His words are,

> *The like natural inducement hath brought men to*
> *know that it is no less their duty, to love others than*
> *themselves; for seeing those things which are equal,*
> *must needs all have one measure; if I cannot but wish*
> *to receive good, even as much at every man's hands,*
> *as any man can wish unto his own soul, how should I*
> *look to have any part of my desire herein satisfied,*
> *unless myself be careful to satisfy the like desire, which*
> *is undoubtedly in other men, being of one and the*
> *same nature? To have any thing offered them repug-*
> *nant to this desire, must needs in all respects grieve*
> *them as much as me; so that if I do harm, I must look*
> *to suffer, there being no reason that others should*
> *shew greater measure of love to me, than they have by*
> *me shewed unto them: my desire therefore to be loved*
> *of my equals in nature, as much as possible may be,*
> *imposeth upon me a natural duty of bearing to them-*
> *ward fully the like affection; from which relation of*
> *equality between ourselves and them that are as our-*
> *selves, what several rules and canons natural reason*
> *hath drawn, for direction of life, no man is ignorant.*
> *Eccl. Pol. Lib. 1.*

§. 6. But though this be *a state of liberty,* yet *it is not a*
state of licence: though man in that state have an uncon-
trollable liberty to dispose of his person or possessions,
yet he has not liberty to destroy himself, or so much as
any creature in his possession, but where some nobler use
than its bare preservation calls for it. The *state of nature*

has a law of nature to govern it, which obliges every one.
And reason, which is that law, teaches all mankind who
will but consult it that, being all *equal and independent,*
no one ought to harm another in his life, health, liberty,
or possessions. For men being all the workmanship of
one omnipotent and infinitely wise maker, all the servants of one sovereign master, sent into the world by his
order and about his business, they are his property whose
workmanship they are,° made to last during his, not one
another's pleasure. And being furnished with like faculties, sharing all in one community of nature, there cannot be supposed any such *subordination* among us that
may authorize us to destroy one another, as if we were
made for one another's uses, as the inferior ranks of creatures are for ours. Every one, as he is *bound to preserve
himself* and not to quit his station willfully, so by the like
reason, when his own preservation comes not in compe-
tition, ought he, as much as he can, *to preserve the rest of
mankind,*° and may not, unless it be to do justice on an
offender, take away, or impair the life, or what tends to
the preservation of the life, the liberty, health, limb, or
goods of another.

§. 7. And that all men may be restrained from invading
others' rights and from doing hurt to one another, and
the law of nature be observed, which wills the peace and
preservation of all mankind, the *execution* of the law of
nature is, in that state, put into every man's hands,
whereby everyone has a right to punish the transgressors
of that law to such a degree as may hinder its violation.°
For the *law of nature* would, as all other laws that concern men in this world, be in vain if there were nobody
that in the state of nature had a *power to execute* that law
and thereby preserve the innocent and restrain offenders.
And if anyone in the state of nature may punish another
for any evil he has done, everyone may do so. For in that

state of perfect equality, where naturally there is no superiority or jurisdiction of one over another, what any may
do in prosecution of that law, everyone must needs have a
right to do.

§. 8. And thus, in the state of nature, *one man comes by a
power over another;* but yet no absolute or arbitrary
power to use a criminal, when he has got him in his
hands, according to the passionate heats or boundless
extravagancy of his own will, but only to retribute to
him, so far as calm reason and conscience dictate, what is
proportionate to his transgression, which is so much as
may serve for *reparation* and *restraint.* For these two are
the only reasons why one man may lawfully do harm to
another, which is that we call *punishment.* In transgressing the law of nature, the offender declares himself to live
by another rule than that of reason and common equity,
which is that measure God has set to the actions of men
for their mutual security; and so he becomes dangerous
to mankind, the tie which is to secure them from injury
and violence being slighted and broken by him. Which,
being a trespass against the whole species and the peace
and safety of it provided for by the law of nature, every
man upon this score, by the right he hath to preserve
mankind in general, may restrain or, where it is necessary, destroy things noxious to them, and so may bring
such evil on anyone who hath transgressed that law as
may make him repent the doing of it and thereby deter
him, and by his example others, from doing the like mischief. And in this case, and upon this ground, *every man
hath a right to punish the offender and be executioner of
the law of nature.*

§. 9. I doubt not but this will seem a very strange doctrine
to some men:° but before they condemn it I desire them
to resolve me by what right any prince or state can put to

death or *punish an alien* for any crime he commits in their country. It is certain their laws, by virtue of any sanction they receive from the promulgated will of the legislative, reach not a stranger. They speak not to him, nor, if they did, is he bound to hearken to them. The legislative authority, by which they are in force over the subjects of that commonwealth, hath no power over him. Those who have the supreme power of making laws in *England, France,* or *Holland* are to an *Indian* but like the rest of the world, men without authority. And therefore, if by the law of nature every man hath not a power to punish offences against it, as he soberly judges the case to require, I see not how the magistrates of any community can *punish an alien* of another country, since, in reference to him, they can have no more power than what every man naturally may have over another.

§. 10. Besides the crime, which consists in violating the law and varying from the right rule of reason, whereby a man so far becomes degenerate and declares himself to quit the principles of human nature and to be a noxious creature, there is commonly *injury* done to some person or other, and some other man receives damage by his transgression; in which case he who hath received any damage has, besides the right of punishment common to him with other men, a particular right to seek *reparation* from him that has done it. And any other person who finds it just may also join with him that is injured and assist him in recovering from the offender so much as may make satisfaction for the harm he has suffered.

§. 11. From these *two distinct rights,* the one of *punishing* the crime *for restraint* and preventing the like offence, which right of punishing is in everybody, the other of taking *reparation,* which belongs only to the injured party, comes it to pass that the magistrate, who by being magistrate hath the common right of punishing put into his hands, can often, where the public good demands not the execution of the law, *remit* the punishment of criminal offences by his own authority, but yet cannot *remit* the satisfaction due to any private man for the damage he has received. That, he who has suffered the damage has a right to demand in his own name, and he alone can remit.° The damnified person has this power of appropriating to himself the goods or service of the offender *by right of self-preservation*, as every man has a power to punish the crime to prevent its being committed again, *by the right he has of preserving all mankind* and doing all reasonable things he can in order to that end. And thus it is that every man, in the state of nature, has a power to kill a murderer, both *to deter* others from doing the like injury, which no reparation can compensate, by the example of the punishment that attends it from everybody, and also to secure men from the attempts of a criminal who, having renounced reason, the common rule and measure God hath given to mankind, hath, by the unjust violence and slaughter he hath committed upon one, declared war against all mankind and therefore may be destroyed as a *lion* or a *tiger*, one of those wild savage beasts with whom men can have no society nor security. And upon this is grounded that great law of nature, *Whoso sheddeth man's blood, by man shall his blood be shed.* And *Cain* was so fully convinced that everyone had a right to destroy such a criminal that, after the murder of his brother, he cries out, *Every one that findeth me, shall slay me,* so plain was it writ in the hearts of all mankind.

§. 12. By the same reason may a man in the state of nature *punish the lesser breaches* of that law. It will perhaps be demanded, with death? I answer, each transgression may be *punished* to that *degree,* and with so much *severity,* as will suffice to make it an ill bargain to the offender, give him cause to repent and terrify others from doing the like. Every offence that can be committed in the state of nature may in the state of nature be also punished, equally and as far forth as it may in a commonwealth. For though it would be besides my present purpose to enter here into the particulars of the law of nature or its *measures of punishment,* yet it is certain there is such a law, and that too, as intelligible and plain to a rational creature and a studier of that law as the positive laws of commonwealths;° nay, possibly plainer, as much as reason is easier to be understood than the fancies and intricate contrivances of men, following contrary and hidden interests put into words. For so truly are a great part of the *municipal laws* of countries, which are only so far right as they are founded on the law of nature, by which they are to be regulated and interpreted.

§. 13. To this strange doctrine, *viz.* that *in the state of nature everyone has the executive power* of the law of nature, I doubt not but it will be objected that it is unreasonable for men to be judges in their own cases, that self-love will make men partial to themselves and their friends, and on the other side, that ill nature, passion and revenge will carry them too far in punishing others. And hence nothing but confusion and disorder will follow and that therefore God hath certainly appointed government to restrain the partiality and violence of men. I easily grant that *civil government* is the proper remedy for the inconveniencies of the state of nature, which must certainly be great where men may be judges in their own case, since it is easy to be imagined that he who was so unjust as to do his brother an injury will scarce be so just as to condemn himself for it. But I shall desire those who make this objection to remember that *absolute monarchs* are but men; and if government is to be the remedy of those evils which necessarily follow from men's being judges in their own cases, and the state of nature is therefore not to be endured, I desire to know what kind of government that is, and how much better it is than the state of nature, where one man, commanding a multitude, has the liberty to be judge in his own case, and may do to all his subjects whatever he pleases, without the least liberty to anyone to question or control those who execute his pleasure, and in whatsoever he doth, whether led by reason, mistake or passion, must be submitted to? Much better it is in the state of nature, wherein men are not bound to submit to the unjust will of another. And if he that judges, judges amiss in his own or any other case, he is answerable for it to the rest of mankind.

§. 14. It is often asked as a mighty objection, *where are or ever were there any men in such a state of nature?* To which it may suffice as an answer at present, that since all princes and rulers of *independent* governments all through the world are in a state of nature, it is plain the world never was, nor ever will be, without numbers of men in that state. I have named all governors of *independent communities*, whether they are, or are not, in league with others. For it is not every compact that puts an end to the state of nature between men, but only this one of agreeing together mutually to enter into one community and make one body politic; other promises and compacts men may make one with another, and yet still be in the state of nature. The promises and bargains for truck, *&c.* between the two men in the desert island, mentioned by *Garcilasso de la Vega* in his history of *Peru,* or between a *Swiss* and an *Indian* in the woods of *America,* are binding to them, though they are perfectly in a state of nature in reference to one another. For truth and keeping of faith belongs to men as men, and not as members of society.

§. 15. To those that say there were never any men in the state of nature, I will not only oppose the authority of the judicious *Hooker, Eccl. Pol. lib.* i. *sect.* 10. where he says, *The laws which have been hitherto mentioned,* i. e. the laws of nature, *do bind men absolutely, even as they are men, although they have never any settled fellowship, never any solemn agreement amongst themselves what to do, or not to do: but forasmuch as we are not by ourselves sufficient to furnish ourselves with competent store of things, needful for such a life as our nature doth desire, a life fit for the dignity of man; therefore to supply those defects and imperfections which are in us, as living single and solely by ourselves, we are naturally induced to seek communion and fellowship with others: this was the cause of men's uniting themselves at first in politic societies.* But I moreover affirm that all men are naturally in that state, and remain so, until by their own consents they make themselves members of some politic society; and I doubt not in the sequel of this discourse to make it very clear.

CHAPTER III

Of the State of War

§. 16. The *state of war* is a state of *enmity* and *destruction*. And therefore declaring by word or action, not a passionate and hasty, but a sedate settled design upon another man's life, *puts him in a state of war* with him against whom he has declared such an intention, and so has exposed his life to the other's power to be taken away by him, or any one that joins with him in his defense and espouses his quarrel; it being reasonable and just, I should have a right to destroy that which threatens me with destruction. For *by the fundamental law of nature, man being to be preserved* as much as possible, when all cannot be preserved, the safety of the innocent is to be preferred. And one may destroy a man who makes war upon him, or has discovered an enmity to his being, for the same reason that he may kill a *wolf* or a *lion:* because such men are not under the ties of the common law of reason, have no other rule but that of force and violence, and so may be treated as beasts of prey, those dangerous and noxious creatures, that will be sure to destroy him whenever he falls into their power.

§. 17. And hence it is that he who attempts to get another man into his absolute power does thereby *put himself into a state of war* with him, it being to be understood as a declaration of a design upon his life. For I have reason to conclude that he who would get me into his power without my consent would use me as he pleased when he had got me there, and destroy me too when he had a fancy to it. For nobody can desire to *have me in his absolute power* unless it be to compel me by force to that which is against the right of my freedom, *i. e.* make me a slave. To be free from such force is the only security of my preservation. And reason bids me look on him as an enemy to my preservation who would take away that *freedom* which is the fence to it, so that he who makes an *attempt to enslave* me thereby puts himself into a state of war with me. He that, in the state of nature, *would take away the freedom* that belongs to any one in that state must necessarily be supposed to have a design to take away everything else, that *freedom* being the foundation of all the rest, as he that, in the state of society, would take away the *freedom* belonging to those of that society or commonwealth must be supposed to design to take away from them everything else, and so be looked on as *in a state of war.*°

§. 18. This makes it lawful for a man to *kill a thief,* who has not in the least hurt him nor declared any design upon his life, any farther than, by the use of force, so to get him in his power as to take away his money, or what he pleases, from him. Because using force where he has no right, to get me into his power, let his pretense be what it will, I have no reason to suppose that he who would *take away my liberty* would not, when he had me in his power, take away everything else. And therefore it is lawful for me to treat him as one who has *put himself into a state of war* with me, *i. e.* kill him if I can; for to that hazard does he justly expose himself, whoever introduces a state of war and is aggressor in it.

§. 19. And here we have the plain *difference between the state of nature and the state of war,* which however some men have confounded, are as far distant as a state of peace, good will, mutual assistance and preservation, and a state of enmity, malice, violence and mutual destruction are one from another. Men living together according to reason, without a common superior on earth with authority to judge between them, is *properly the state of nature.* But force, or a declared design of force, upon the person of another, where there is no common superior on earth to appeal to for relief, *is the state of war;* and it is the want of such an appeal gives a man the right of war even against an *aggressor,* though he be in society and a fellow subject. Thus a *thief,* whom I cannot harm but by appeal to the law for having stolen all that I am worth, I may kill when he sets on me to rob me but of my horse or coat. Because the law, which was made for my preservation, where it cannot interpose to secure my life from present force, which, if lost is capable of no reparation, permits me my own defense and the right of war, a liberty to kill the aggressor, because the aggressor allows not time to appeal to our common judge nor the decision of the law for remedy in a case where the mischief may be irreparable. Want of a common judge with authority puts all men in a state of nature. Force without right upon a man's person makes a state of war, both where there is and is not a common judge.

§. 20. But when the actual force is over, the *state of war ceases* between those that are in society, and are equally on both sides subjected to the fair determination of the law; because then there lies open the remedy of appeal for the past injury and to prevent future harm. But where no such appeal is, as in the state of nature, for want of positive laws and judges with authority to appeal to, the state of war once begun, continues, with a right to the innocent party to destroy the other whenever he can, until the aggressor offers peace and desires reconciliation on such terms as may repair any wrongs he has already done and secure the innocent for the future. Nay, where an appeal to the law and constituted judges lies open, but the remedy is denied by a manifest perverting of justice and a barefaced wresting of the laws to protect or indemnify the violence or injuries of some men or party of men, *there* it is hard to imagine anything but *a state of war*. For wherever violence is used and injury done, though by hands appointed to administer justice, it is still violence and injury, however coloured with the name, pretenses, or forms of law, the end whereof being to protect and redress the innocent, by an unbiased application of it to all who are under it. Wherever that is not *bona fide* done, *war is made* upon the sufferers, who, having no appeal on earth to right them, they are left to the only remedy in such cases, an appeal to heaven.

§. 21. To avoid this *state of war* (wherein there is no appeal but to heaven and wherein every the least difference is apt to end, where there is no authority to decide between the contenders) is one great reason of men's putting themselves into society and quitting the state of nature. For where there is an authority, a power on earth, from which relief can be had by *appeal*, there the continuance of the *state of war* is excluded and the controversy is decided by that power. Had there been any such court, any superior jurisdiction on earth, to determine the right between *Jephtha* and the *Ammonites,* they had never come to a *state of war;* but we see he was forced to appeal to heaven.

The Lord the Judge (says he) *be judge this day between the children of* Israel *and the children of* Ammon, *Judg.* xi. 27. And then prosecuting and relying on his *appeal,* he leads out his army to battle. And therefore in such controversies, where the question is put, *who shall be judge?,* it cannot be meant, who shall decide the controversy. Everyone knows what *Jephtha* here tells us, that *the Lord the Judge* shall judge. Where there is no judge on earth the appeal lies to God in heaven. That question then cannot mean, who shall judge whether another hath put himself in a *state of war* with me and whether I may, as *Jephtha* did, *appeal to heaven* in it? Of that I myself can only be judge in my own conscience, as I will answer it, at the great day, to the supreme judge of all men.

CHAPTER IV

Of Slavery

§. 22. The *natural liberty* of man is to be free from any superior power on earth and not to be under the will or legislative authority of man, but to have only the law of nature for his rule. The *liberty of man* in society is to be under no other legislative power but that established, by consent, in the commonwealth, nor under the dominion of any will or restraint of any law but what that legislative shall enact, according to the trust put in it. Freedom then is not what Sir *Robert Filmer* tells us, *Observations, A. 55.° a liberty for everyone to do what he lists, to live as he pleases, and not to be tied by any laws.* But *freedom of men under government* is to have a standing rule to live by, common to everyone of that society and made by the legislative power erected in it, a liberty to follow my own will in all things where the rule prescribes not, and not to be subject to the inconstant, uncertain, unknown, arbitrary will of another man. As *freedom of nature* is to be under no other restraint but the law of nature.

§. 23. This *freedom* from absolute, arbitrary power is so necessary to, and closely joined with, a man's preservation that he cannot part with it but by what forfeits his preservation and life together. For a man, not having the power of his own life, *cannot,* by compact or his own consent, *enslave himself* to anyone nor put himself under the absolute, arbitrary power of another, to take away his life when he pleases.° Nobody can give more power than he has himself; and he that cannot take away his own life cannot give another power over it. Indeed, having by his fault forfeited his own life by some act that deserves death, he to whom he has forfeited it may (when he has him in his power) delay to take it and make use of him to his own service, and he does him no injury by it. For whenever he finds the hardship of his slavery outweigh the value of his life, it is in his power, by resisting the will of his master, to draw on himself the death he desires.

§. 24. This is the perfect condition of *slavery,* which is nothing else but *the state of war continued between a lawful conqueror and a captive.* For if once *compact* enter between them and make an agreement for a limited power on the one side and obedience on the other, the *state of war and slavery* ceases, as long as the compact endures. For, as has been said, no man can, by agreement, pass over to another that which he hath not in himself, a power over his own life.

I confess we find among the *Jews,* as well as other nations, that men did sell themselves; but it is plain this was only to *drudgery, not to slavery.* For it is evident the person sold was not under an absolute, arbitrary, despotical power. For the master could not have power to kill him, at any time, whom, at a certain time, he was obliged to let go free out of his service; and the master of such a servant was so far from having an arbitrary power over his life, that he could not, at pleasure, so much as maim him, but the loss of an eye, or tooth, set him free, *Exod.* xxi.°

CHAPTER V

Of Property

§. 25. Whether we consider natural *reason*, which tells us that men, being once born, have a right to their preservation, and consequently to meat and drink and such other things as nature affords for their subsistence, or *revelation*, which gives us an account of those grants God made of the world to *Adam*, and to *Noah*, and his sons: it is very clear that God, as King *David* says, *Psal.* CXV. 16. *has given the earth to the children of men*, given it to mankind in common. But this being supposed, it seems to some a very great difficulty how anyone should ever come to have a *property* in any thing. I will not content myself to answer that if it be difficult to make out *property*, upon a supposition that God gave the world to *Adam* and his posterity in common, it is impossible that any man but one universal monarch should have any *property* upon a supposition that God gave the world to *Adam* and his heirs in succession, exclusive of all the rest of his posterity.° But I shall endeavour to show how men might come to have a *property* in several parts of that which God gave to mankind in common, and that without any express compact of all the commoners.

§. 26. God, who hath given the world to men in common, hath also given them reason to make use of it to the best advantage of life and convenience. The earth and all that is therein is given to men for the support and comfort of their being. And though all the fruits it naturally produces and beasts it feeds belong to mankind in common, as they are produced by the spontaneous hand of nature, and nobody has originally a private dominion, exclusive of the rest of mankind, in any of them as they are thus in their natural state, yet, being given for the use of men, there must of necessity be *a means to appropriate* them some way or other before they can be of any use or at all beneficial to any particular man. The fruit or venison which nourishes the wild *Indian,* who knows no enclosure and is still a tenant in common, must be his, and so his, *i. e.* a part of him, that another can no longer have any right to it, before it can do him any good for the support of his life.

§. 27. Though the earth and all inferior creatures be common to all men, yet every man has a *property* in his own *person.* This nobody has any right to but himself. The *labour* of his body and the *work* of his hands, we may say, are properly his. Whatsoever then he removes out of the state that nature hath provided and left it in, he hath mixed his *labour* with and joined to it something that is his own, and thereby makes it his *property.*° It being by him removed from the common state nature hath placed it in, it hath by this *labour* something annexed to it that excludes the common right of other men. For this *labour* being the unquestionable property of the labourer, no man but he can have a right to what that is once joined to, at least where there is enough, and as good, left in common for others.°

§. 28. He that is nourished by the acorns he picked up under an oak or the apples he gathered from the trees in the wood has certainly appropriated them to himself. Nobody can deny but the nourishment is his. I ask then, when did they begin to be his? When he digested? Or when he ate? Or when he boiled? Or when he brought them home? Or when he picked them up? And it is plain, if the first gathering made them not his, nothing else could. That *labour* put a distinction between them and common. That added something to them more than nature, the common mother of all, had done. And so they became his private right.° And will anyone say he had no right to those acorns or apples he thus appropriated because he had not the consent of all mankind to make them his? Was it a robbery thus to assume to himself what belonged to all in common? If such a consent as that was necessary man had starved, notwithstanding the plenty God had given him. We see in *commons* which remain so by compact that it is the taking any part of what is common, and removing it out of the state nature leaves it in, which *begins the property,* without which the common is of no use. And the taking of this or that part does not depend on the express consent of all the commoners. Thus the grass my horse has bit, the turfs my servant has cut, and the ore I have dug, in any place where I have a right to them in common with others, become my *property,* without the assignation or consent of any body. The *labour* that was mine, removing them out of that common state they were in, hath *fixed* my *property* in them.

§. 29. By making an explicit consent of every commoner necessary to anyone's appropriating to himself any part of what is given in common, children or servants could not cut the meat which their father or master had provided for them in common, without assigning to everyone his peculiar part. Though the water running in the fountain be everyone's, yet who can doubt but that in the pitcher is his only who drew it out? His *labour* hath taken it out of the hands of nature, where it was common and belonged equally to all her children, and *hath* thereby *appropriated* it to himself.

§. 30. Thus this law of reason makes the deer that *Indian*'s who hath killed it; it is allowed to be his goods who hath bestowed his labour upon it, though before it was the common right of everyone. And amongst those who are counted the civilized part of mankind, who have made and multiplied positive laws to determine *property*, this original law of nature for the *beginning of property*, in what was before common, still takes place. And by virtue thereof, what fish any one catches in the ocean, that great and still remaining common of mankind, or what ambergrise any one takes up here, is, by the *labour* that removes it out of that common state nature left it in, *made* his *property* who takes those pains about it. And even amongst us, the hare that any one is hunting is thought his who pursues her during the chase. For being a beast that is still looked upon as common and no man's private possession, whoever has employed so much *labour* about any of that kind as to find and pursue her has thereby removed her from the state of nature, wherein she was common, and hath *begun a property*.

§. 31. It will perhaps be objected to this that if gathering the acorns or other fruits of the earth, *&c.* makes a right to them, then anyone may *engross* as much as he will. To which I answer, not so. The same law of nature that does by this means give us property, does also *bound* that

property too. *God has given us all things richly,* 1 Tim. vi.
12. is the voice of reason confirmed by inspiration. But
how far has he given it us? *To enjoy.* As much as anyone
can make use of to any advantage of life before it spoils,
so much he may by his labour fix a property in. Whatever
is beyond this is more than his share and belongs to
others.° Nothing was made by God for man to spoil or
destroy. And thus, considering the plenty of natural provisions there was a long time in the world and the few
spenders, and to how small a part of that provision the
industry of one man could extend itself and engross it to
the prejudice of others, especially keeping within the
bounds set by reason of what might serve for his *use,*
there could be then little room for quarrels or conten-
tions about property so established.

§. 32. But the *chief matter of property* being now not the
fruits of the earth and the beasts that subsist on it, but *the
earth itself,* as that which takes in and carries with it all
the rest, I think it is plain that *property* in that too is
acquired as the former. *As much land* as a man tills,
plants, improves, cultivates, and can use the product of,
so much is his *property.* He by his labour does, as it were,
enclose it from the common. Nor will it invalidate his
right to say everybody else has an equal title to it, and
therefore he cannot appropriate, he cannot enclose, without the consent of all his fellow commoners, all mankind.
God, when he gave the world in common to all mankind,
commanded man also to labour, and the penury of his
condition required it of him. God and his reason commanded him to subdue the earth, *i. e.* improve it for the
benefit of life, and therein lay out something upon it that
was his own, his labour. He that in obedience to this
command of God subdued, tilled and sowed any part of
it, thereby annexed to it something that was his *property,*

which another had no title to nor could without injury take from him.

§. 33. Nor was this *appropriation* of any parcel of *land*, by improving it, any prejudice to any other man, since there was still enough and as good left, and more than the yet unprovided could use. So that, in effect, there was never the less left for others because of his enclosure for himself. For he that leaves as much as another can make use of, does as good as take nothing at all. Nobody could think himself injured by the drinking of another man, though he took a good draught, who had a whole river of the same water left him to quench his thirst. And the case of land and water, where there is enough of both, is perfectly the same.

§. 34. God gave the world to men in common. But since he gave it to them for their benefit and the greatest conveniencies of life they were capable to draw from it, it cannot be supposed he meant it should always remain common and uncultivated. He gave it to the use of the industrious and rational (and *labour* was to be *his title* to it), not to the fancy or covetousness of the quarrelsome and contentious. He that had as good left for his improvement as was already taken up, needed not complain, ought not to meddle with what was already improved by another's labour. If he did, it is plain he desired the benefit of another's pains, which he had no right to, and not the ground which God had given him in common with others to labour on, and whereof there was as good left as that already possessed, and more than he knew what to do with or his industry could reach to.

§. 35. It is true in *land* that is *common* in *England* or any other country, where there is plenty of people under government who have money and commerce, no one can enclose or appropriate any part without the consent of all his fellow commoners, because this is left common by compact, *i. e.* by the law of the land, which is not to be violated. And though it be common in respect of some men, it is not so to all mankind, but is the joint property of this country or this parish. Besides, the remainder, after such enclosure, would not be as good to the rest of the commoners as the whole was when they could all make use of the whole; whereas in the beginning and first peopling of the great common of the world it was quite otherwise. The law man was under was rather for appropriating. God commanded, and his wants forced him, to *labour*. That was his *property* which could not be taken from him wherever he had fixed it. And hence subduing or cultivating the earth, and having dominion, we see are joined together. The one gave title to the other. So that God, by commanding to subdue, gave authority so far to *appropriate*. And the condition of human life, which requires labour and materials to work on, necessarily introduces private possessions.

§. 36. The *measure of property* nature has well set by the extent of men's *labour and the conveniencies of life:* no man's labour could subdue or appropriate all, nor could his enjoyment consume more than a small part. So that it was impossible for any man, this way, to entrench upon the right of another, or acquire to himself a property to the prejudice of his neighbour, who would still have room for as good and as large a possession (after the other had taken out his) as before it was appropriated. This *measure* did confine every man's *possession* to a very moderate proportion, and such as he might appropriate to himself without injury to anybody, in the first ages of the world, when men were more in danger to be lost by wandering from their company in the then vast wilderness of the earth, than to be straitened for want of room to plant in.

And the same *measure* may be allowed still without prejudice to anybody, as full as the world seems. For supposing a man or family, in the state they were at first peopling of the world by the children of *Adam* or *Noah*: let him plant in some inland, vacant places of *America*, we shall find that the *possessions* he could make himself, upon the *measures* we have given, would not be very large, nor, even to this day, prejudice the rest of mankind or give them reason to complain or think themselves injured by this man's encroachment, though the race of men have now spread themselves to all the corners of the world and do infinitely exceed the small number which was at the beginning. Nay, the extent of *ground* is of so little value *without labour*, that I have heard it affirmed that in *Spain* itself a man may be permitted to plough, sow and reap, without being disturbed, upon land he has no other title to but only his making use of it. But, on the contrary, the inhabitants think themselves beholden to him, who, by his industry on neglected and consequently waste land, has increased the stock of corn, which they wanted. But be this as it will, which I lay no stress on, this I dare boldly affirm: that the same *rule of property*, (*viz.*) that every man should have as much as he could make use of, would hold still in the world without straitening anybody, since there is land enough in the world to suffice double the inhabitants, had not the *invention of money*, and the tacit agreement of men to put a value on it, introduced (by consent) larger possessions, and a right to them; which, how it has done, I shall by and by show more at large.°

§. 37. This is certain, that in the beginning, before the desire of having more than man needed had altered the intrinsic value of things, which depends only on their usefulness to the life of man, or had *agreed that a little piece of yellow metal*, which would keep without wasting or decay, should be worth a great piece of flesh or a whole heap of corn: though men had a right to appropriate by their labour, each one to himself, as much of the things of nature as he could use, yet this could not be much, nor to the prejudice of others, where the same plenty was still left to those who would use the same industry. To which let me add, that he who appropriates land to himself by his labour does not lessen, but increase, the common stock of mankind. For the provisions serving to the support of human life produced by one acre of enclosed and cultivated land are (to speak much within compass) ten times more than those which are yielded by an acre of land of an equal richness lying waste in common. And therefore he that encloses land, and has a greater plenty of the conveniencies of life from ten acres than he could have from an hundred left to nature, may truly be said to give ninety acres to mankind. For his labour now supplies him with provisions out of ten acres which were but the product of an hundred lying in common. I have here rated the improved land very low in making its product but as ten to one, when it is much nearer an hundred to one. For I ask whether in the wild woods and uncultivated waste of *America,* left to nature without any improvement, tillage or husbandry, a thousand acres yield the needy and wretched inhabitants as many conveniencies of life as ten acres of equally fertile land do in *Devonshire,* where they are well cultivated?

Before the appropriation of land, he who gathered as much of the wild fruit, killed, caught, or tamed, as many of the beasts, as he could, he that so employed his pains about any of the spontaneous products of nature as any way to alter them from the state which nature put them in, *by* placing any of his *labour* on them, did thereby *acquire a propriety in them.* But if they perished in his possession without their due use, if the fruits rotted or the venison putrified before he could spend it, he offended against the common law of nature and was liable to be punished. He invaded his neighbour's share, for he had *no right farther than his use* called for any of them and they might serve to afford him conveniencies of life.

§. 38. The same *measures* governed the *possession of land* too: whatsoever he tilled and reaped, laid up and made use of, before it spoiled, that was his peculiar right; whatsoever he enclosed, and could feed, and make use of, the cattle and product was also his. But if either the grass of his enclosure rotted on the ground or the fruit of his planting perished without gathering and laying up, this part of the earth, notwithstanding his enclosure, was still to be looked on as waste and might be the possession of any other. Thus, at the beginning, *Cain* might take as much ground as he could till and make it his own land, and yet leave enough to *Abel*'s sheep to feed on; a few acres would serve for both their possessions. But as families increased and industry enlarged their stocks, their *possessions enlarged* with the need of them; but yet it was commonly *without any fixed property in the ground* they made use of until they incorporated, settled themselves together, and built cities. And then, by consent, they came in time to set out the *bounds of their distinct territories* and agree on limits between them and their neighbours, and by laws within themselves settled the *properties* of those of the same society. For we see that in that part of the world which was first inhabited, and therefore like to be best peopled, even as low down as *Abraham*'s time, they wandered with their flocks and their herds, which was their substance, freely up and down; and this *Abraham* did in a country where he was a stranger. Whence it is plain that at least a great part of the *land lay in common,* that the inhabitants valued it not, nor claimed property in any more than they made use of. But when there was not room enough in the same place for their herds to feed together, they by consent, as *Abraham* and

Lot did, *Gen.* xiii. 5., separated and enlarged their pasture where it best liked them. And for the same reason *Esau* went from his father and his brother and planted in *Mount Seir, Gen.* xxxvi. 6.

§. 39. And thus, without supposing any private dominion and property in *Adam* over all the world, exclusive of all other men, which can no way be proved nor any one's property be made out from it; but supposing the *world* given, as it was, to the children of men *in common,* we see how *labour* could make men distinct titles to several parcels of it for their private uses, wherein there could be no doubt of right, no room for quarrel.

§. 40. Nor is it so strange, as perhaps before consideration it may appear, that the *property of labour* should be able to over-balance the community of land. For it is *labour* indeed that *puts the difference of value* on everything. And let anyone consider what the difference is between an acre of land planted with tobacco or sugar, sown with wheat or barley, and an acre of the same land lying in common without any husbandry upon it, and he will find that the improvement of *labour makes* the far greater part of the value. I think it will be but a very modest computation to say that of the *products* of the earth useful to the life of man, nine tenths are the *effects of labour:* nay, if we will rightly estimate things as they come to our use and cast up the several expenses about them, what in them is purely owing to *nature* and what to *labour,* we shall find that in most of them ninety-nine hundredths are wholly to be put on the account of *labour.*°

§. 41. There cannot be a clearer demonstration of anything than several nations of the *Americans* are of this, who are rich in land and poor in all the comforts of life, whom nature having furnished as liberally as any other people with the materials of plenty, *i. e.* a fruitful soil, apt to produce in abundance, what might serve for food, raiment, and delight; yet for *want of improving it by labour* have not one hundredth part of the conveniencies we enjoy. And a king of a large and fruitful territory there, feeds, lodges, and is clad worse than a day labourer in *England.*

§. 42. To make this a little clearer, let us but trace some of the ordinary provisions of life through their several progresses, before they come to our use, and see how much they receive of their *value from human industry.* Bread, wine and cloth are things of daily use and great plenty; yet notwithstanding, acorns, water and leaves, or skins, must be our bread, drink and clothing, did not *labour* furnish us with these more useful commodities. For whatever *bread* is more worth than acorns, wine than water, and *cloth* or *silk* than leaves, skins or moss, that is wholly *owing to labour* and *industry.* The one of these being the food and raiment which unassisted nature furnishes us with, the other provisions which our industry and pains prepare for us, which how much they exceed the other in value, when anyone hath computed, he will then see how much *labour makes the far greatest part of the value* of things we enjoy in this world. And the ground which produces the materials is scarce to be reckoned in as any, or at most but a very small part of it, so little that even amongst us, land that is left wholly to nature, that hath no improvement of pasturage, tillage, or planting, is called, as indeed it is, *waste;* and we shall find the benefit of it amount to little more than nothing. This shows how much numbers of men are to be preferred to largeness of dominions, and that the increase of lands and the right employing of them is the great art of government. And that prince who shall be so wise and godlike as by established laws of liberty to secure protection and encouragement to the honest industry of mankind, against the oppression of power and narrowness of party, will quickly be too hard for his neighbours. But this by the by. To return to the argument in hand:

§. 43. An acre of land that bears here twenty bushels of wheat, and another in *America*, which, with the same husbandry, would do the like, are, without doubt, of the same natural intrinsic value. But yet the benefit mankind receives from the one in a year is worth 5 *l.* and from the other possibly not worth a penny, if all the profit an *Indian* received from it were to be valued and sold here; at least, I may truly say, not one thousandth. It is *labour* then which *puts the greatest part of value upon land,* without which it would scarcely be worth anything; it is to that we owe the greatest part of all its useful products. For all that the straw, bran, bread, of that acre of wheat, is more worth than the product of an acre of as good land which lies waste, is all the effect of labour. For it is not barely the ploughman's pains, the reaper's and thresher's toil, and the baker's sweat, is to be counted into the *bread* we eat. The labour of those who broke the oxen, who digged and wrought the iron and stones, who felled and framed the timber employed about the plough, mill, oven, or any other utensils, which are a vast number, requisite to this corn, from its being seed to be sown to its being made bread, must all be *charged on* the account of *labour* and received as an effect of that. Nature and the earth furnished only the almost worthless materials, as in themselves. It would be a strange *catalogue of things that industry provided and made use of, about every loaf of bread,* before it came to our use, if we could trace them: iron, wood, leather, bark, timber, stone, bricks, coals, lime, cloth, dying drugs, pitch, tar, masts, ropes, and all the materials made use of in the ship that brought any of the commodities made use of by any of the workmen to any part of the work; all which it would be almost impossible, at least too long, to reckon up.

§. 44. From all which it is evident that though the things of nature are given in common, yet man, by being master of himself and *proprietor of his own person and the actions or labour of it, had still in himself the great foundation of property.* And that which made up the great part of what he applied to the support or comfort of his being, when invention and arts had improved the conveniencies of life, was perfectly his own and did not belong in common to others.

§. 45. Thus *labour,* in the beginning, *gave a right of property* wherever anyone was pleased to employ it upon what was common, which remained a long while the far greater part and is yet more than mankind makes use of. Men at first, for the most part, contented themselves with what unassisted nature offered to their necessities. And though afterwards in some parts of the world (where the increase of people and stock, with the *use of money,* had made land scarce and so of some value) the several *communities* settled the bounds of their distinct territories and by laws within themselves regulated the properties of the private men of their society, and so, *by compact* and agreement, *settled the property* which labour and industry began. And the leagues that have been made between several states and kingdoms, either expressly or tacitly disowning all claim and right to the land in the others possession, have, by common consent, given up their pretenses to their natural common right, which originally they had to those countries, and so have, by *positive agreement, settled a property* amongst themselves in distinct parts and parcels of the earth.° Yet there are still *great tracts of ground* to be found which (the inhabitants thereof not having joined with the rest of mankind in the consent of the use of their common money) *lie waste* and are more than the people who dwell on it do or can make use of, and so still lie in common; though this can scarce happen amongst that part of mankind that have consented to the use of money.

§. 46. The greatest part of *things really useful* to the life of man, and such as the necessity of subsisting made the first commoners of the world look after, as it does the *Americans* now, *are* generally things of *short duration,* such as, if they are not consumed by use, will decay and perish of themselves. Gold, silver and diamonds are things that fancy or agreement hath put the value on, more than real use and the necessary support of life. Now of those good things which nature hath provided in common, everyone had a right (as hath been said) to as much as he could use and *property* in all that he could effect with his labour; all that his *industry* could extend to, to alter from the state nature had put it in, was his. He that *gathered* a hundred bushels of acorns or apples had thereby a *property* in them, they were his goods as soon as gathered. He was only to look that he used them before they spoiled, else he took more than his share and robbed others. And indeed it was a foolish thing, as well as dishonest, to hoard up more than he could make use of. If he gave away a part to anybody else, so that it perished not uselessly in his possession, these he also made use of. And if he also bartered away plums, that would have rotted in a week, for nuts that would last good for his eating a whole year, he did no injury; he wasted not the common stock, destroyed no part of the portion of goods that belonged to others, so long as nothing perished uselessly in his hands. Again, if he would give his nuts for a piece of metal, pleased with its colour, or exchange his sheep for shells, or wool for a sparkling pebble or a diamond, and keep those by him all his life, he invaded not the

right of others. He might heap up as much of these dura-
ble things as he pleased, the *exceeding of the bounds of* his
just property not lying in the largeness of his possession,
but the perishing of anything uselessly in it.°

§. 47. And thus *came in the use of money,* some lasting
thing that men might keep without spoiling, and that by
mutual consent men would take in exchange for the truly
useful, but perishable, supports of life.

§. 48. And as different degrees of industry were apt to
give men possessions in different proportions, so this
invention of money gave them the opportunity to continue and enlarge them. For supposing an island, separate from all possible commerce with the rest of the
world, wherein there were but an hundred families, but
there were sheep, horses and cows, with other useful animals, wholesome fruits, and land enough for corn for a
hundred thousand times as many, but nothing in the
island, either because of its commonness or perishable-
ness, fit to supply the place of *money:* what reason could
anyone have there to enlarge his possessions beyond the
use of his family, and a plentiful supply to its *consump-
tion,* either in what their own industry produced or they
could barter for like perishable, useful commodities with
others? Where there is not some thing, both lasting and
scarce and so valuable to be hoarded up, there men will
not be apt to enlarge their *possessions of land,* were it
never so rich, never so free for them to take. For I ask,
what would a man value ten thousand or an hundred
thousand acres of excellent *land,* ready cultivated and
well stocked too with cattle, in the middle of the inland
parts of *America,* where he had no hopes of commerce
with other parts of the world to draw *money* to him by
the sale of the product? It would not be worth the enclos-
ing, and we should see him give up again to the wild

common of nature whatever was more than would supply the conveniencies of life to be had there for him and his family.

§. 49. Thus in the beginning all the world was *America,* and more so than that is now; for no such thing as *money* was anywhere known. Find out something that hath the *use and value of money* amongst his neighbours, you shall see the same man will begin presently to enlarge his possessions.

§. 50. But since gold and silver, being little useful to the life of man in proportion to food, raiment, and carriage, has its *value* only from the consent of men, whereof *labour* yet *makes,* in great part, *the measure:* it is plain that men have agreed to a disproportionate and unequal *possession of the earth,* they having, by a tacit and voluntary consent, found out a way how a man may fairly possess more land than he himself can use the product of, by receiving in exchange for the overplus gold and silver, which may be hoarded up without injury to anyone, these metals not spoiling or decaying in the hands of the possessor. This partage of things in an inequality of private possessions men have made practicable out of the bounds of society, and without compact, only by putting a value on gold and silver and tacitly agreeing in the use of money. For in governments the laws regulate the right of property, and the possession of land is determined by positive constitutions.

§. 51. And thus, I think, it is very easy to conceive without any difficulty *how labour could at first begin a title of property* in the common things of nature and how the spending it upon our uses bounded it. So that there could then be no reason of quarrelling about title, nor any doubt about the largeness of possession it gave. Right and conveniency went together; for as a man had a right to all he could employ his labour upon, so he had no temptation to labour for more than he could make use of. This left no room for controversy about the title, nor for encroachment on the right of others; what portion a man carved to himself was easily seen, and it was useless, as well as dishonest, to carve himself too much or take more than he needed.

CHAPTER VI

Of Paternal Power

§. 52. It may perhaps be censured, as an impertinent criticism in a discourse of this nature, to find fault with words and names that have obtained in the world. And yet possibly it may not be amiss to offer new ones, when the old are apt to lead men into mistakes, as this of *paternal power* probably has done, which seems so to place the power of parents over their children wholly in the *father,* as if the *mother* had no share in it;° whereas, if we consult reason or revelation, we shall find she hath an equal title. This may give one reason to ask whether this might not be more properly called *parental power?* For whatever obligation nature and the right of generation lays on children, it must certainly bind them equally to both the concurrent causes of it. And accordingly we see the positive law of God everywhere joins them together, without distinction, when it commands the obedience of children, *Honour thy father and thy mother,* Exod. xx. 12. *Whosoever curseth his father or his mother,* Lev. xx. 9. *Ye shall*

fear every man his mother and his father, Lev. xix. 3.
Children, obey your parents, &c. Eph. vi. 1. is the style of
the Old and New Testament.

§. 53. Had but this one thing been well considered, without looking any deeper into the matter, it might perhaps
have kept men from running into those gross mistakes
they have made about this power of parents; which however it might, without any great harshness, bear the name
of absolute dominion and regal authority, when under
the title of *paternal power* it seemed appropriated to the
father, would yet have sounded but oddly, and in the very
name shown the absurdity, if this supposed absolute
power over children had been called *parental,* and
thereby have discovered that it belonged to the *mother*
too. For it will but very ill serve the turn of those men
who contend so much for the absolute power and authority of the *fatherhood,* as they call it, that the mother
should have any share in it. And it would have but ill supported the *monarchy* they contend for when, by the very
name, it appeared that that fundamental authority from
whence they would derive their government of a single
person only, was not placed in one, but two persons
jointly. But to let this of names pass.

§. 54. Though I have said above, *Chap.* II. *That all men by
nature are equal,* I cannot be supposed to understand all
sorts of *equality:* *age* or *virtue* may give men a just prece-
dency; *excellency of parts* and *merit* may place others
above the common level; *birth* may subject some, and
alliance or *benefits* others, to pay an observance to those
to whom nature, gratitude, or other respects may have
made it due. And yet all this consists with the *equality*
which all men are in, in respect of jurisdiction or dominion one over another, which was the *equality* I there
spoke of as proper to the business in hand, being that

equal right that every man hath *to his natural freedom,* without being subjected to the will or authority of any other man.

§. 55. *Children,* I confess, are not born in this full state of *equality,* though they are born to it.° Their parents have a sort of rule and jurisdiction over them when they come into the world and for some time after; but it is but a temporary one. The bonds of this subjection are like the swaddling clothes they are wrapped up in and supported by in the weakness of their infancy. Age and reason as they grow up loosen them, until at length they drop quite off and leave a man at his own free disposal.

§. 56. *Adam* was created a perfect man, his body and mind in full possession of their strength and reason, and so was capable from the first instant of his being to provide for his own support and preservation and govern his actions according to the dictates of the law of reason which God had implanted in him. From him the world is peopled with his descendants, who are all born infants, weak and helpless, without knowledge or understanding. But to supply the defects of this imperfect state, until the improvement of growth and age hath removed them, *Adam* and *Eve,* and after them all *parents,* were, by the law of nature, *under an obligation to preserve, nourish, and educate the children* they had begotten, not as their own workmanship, but the workmanship of their own maker, the Almighty,° to whom they were to be accountable for them.°

§. 57. The law that was to govern *Adam* was the same that was to govern all his posterity, the *law of reason.* But his offspring having another way of entrance into the world, different from him, by a natural birth that produced them ignorant and without the use of *reason,* they were not presently *under that law;* for nobody can be under a law which is not promulgated to him. And this law being promulgated or made known by *reason* only, he that is not come to the use of his *reason* cannot be said to be *under this law;* and *Adam*'s children, being not presently as soon as born *under this law of reason,* were not presently *free.* For *law,* in its true notion, *is* not so much the limitation as *the direction of a free and intelligent agent* to his proper interest and prescribes no farther than is for the general good of those under that law. Could they be happier without it the *law,* as a useless thing, would of itself vanish; and that ill deserves the name of confinement which hedges us in only from bogs and precipices. So that, however it may be mistaken, *the end of law is* not to abolish or restrain, but *to preserve and enlarge freedom:* for in all the states of created beings capable of laws, *where there is no law, there is no freedom.* For *liberty* is to be free from restraint and violence from others, which cannot be where there is no law. But freedom is not, as we are told, *a liberty for every man to do what he lists*° (for who could be free when every other man's humour might domineer over him?), but a *liberty* to dispose and order as he lists his person, actions, possessions, and his whole property, within the allowance of those laws under which he is, and therein not to be subject to the arbitrary will of another, but freely follow his own.

§. 58. The *power,* then, *that parents have* over their children arises from that duty which is incumbent on them to take care of their offspring during the imperfect state of childhood. To inform the mind and govern the actions of their yet ignorant nonage, until reason shall take its place and ease them of that trouble, is what the children want and the parents are bound to. For God having given man an understanding to direct his actions, has allowed him a freedom of will and liberty of acting, as properly belonging thereunto, within the bounds of that law he is under. But whilst he is in an estate wherein he has not *understanding* of his own to direct his *will,* he is not to have any *will* of his own to follow. He that *understands* for him must *will* for him too, he must prescribe to his will and regulate his actions; but when he comes to the estate that made his *father a freeman,* the *son is a freeman* too.

§. 59. This holds in all the laws a man is under, whether natural or civil. Is a man under the law of nature? *What made him free* of that law? What gave him a free disposing of his property, according to his own will, within the compass of that law? I answer, a state of maturity wherein he might be supposed capable to know that law, that so he might keep his actions within the bounds of it. When he has acquired that state he is presumed to know how far that law is to be his guide and how far he may make use of his *freedom,* and so comes to have it; until then somebody else must guide him who is presumed to know how far the law allows a liberty. If such a state of reason, such an age of discretion *made him free,* the same shall make his son free too. Is a man under the law of *England? What made him free* of that law, that is, to have the liberty to dispose of his actions and possessions according to his own will, within the permission of that law? A capacity of knowing that law, which is supposed by that law at the age of one and twenty years, and in some cases sooner. If this *made* the father *free,* it shall *make* the son *free* too. Until then we see the law allows the son to have no will, but he is to be guided by the will of his father or guardian, who is to understand for him. And if the father die and fail to substitute a deputy in his trust, if he hath not provided a tutor to govern his son during his minority, during his want of understanding, the law takes care to do it. Some other must govern him and be a will to him until he hath *attained to a state of freedom* and his under-standing be fit to take the government of his will. But after that, the father and son are equally *free* as much as tutor and pupil after nonage, equally subjects of the same law together, without any dominion left in the father over the life, liberty, or estate of his son, whether they be only in the state and under the law of nature or under the positive laws of an established government.

§. 60. But if, through defects that may happen out of the ordinary course of nature, anyone comes not to such a degree of reason wherein he might be supposed capable of knowing the law and so living within the rules of it, he is *never capable of being a free man,* he is never let loose to the disposure of his own will (because he knows no bounds to it, has not understanding, its proper guide), but is continued under the tuition and government of others, all the time his own understanding is incapable of that charge. And so *lunatics* and *idiots* are never set free from the government of their parents; *children, who are not as yet come unto those years whereat they may have, and innocents which are excluded by a natural defect from ever having;* thirdly, *madmen, which for the present cannot possibly have the use of right reason to guide themselves, have for their guide the reason that guideth other men which are tutors over them, to seek and procure their good for them,* says Hooker, Eccl. Pol. *lib.* i. *sect.* 7. All which seems no more than that duty which God and nature has laid on man, as well as other creatures, to preserve their offspring until they can be able to shift for themselves, and will scarce amount to an instance or proof of *parents'* regal authority.

§. 61. Thus we are *born free* as we are born rational, not that we have actually the exercise of either: age, that brings one, brings with it the other too. And thus we see how *natural freedom and subjection to parents* may consist together and are both founded on the same principle. A *child* is *free* by his father's title, by his father's understanding, which is to govern him until he hath it of his own. The *freedom of a man at years of discretion,* and the *subjection* of a child *to* his *parents,* whilst yet short of that age, are so consistent and so distinguishable that the most blinded contenders for monarchy *by right of fatherhood* cannot miss this *difference;* the most obstinate cannot but allow their consistency. For were their doctrine all true, were the right heir of *Adam* now known and by that title settled a monarch in his throne, invested with all the absolute unlimited power Sir *Robert Filmer* talks of, if he should die as soon as his heir were born, must not the *child,* notwithstanding he were never so free, never so much sovereign, be in subjection to his mother and nurse, to tutors and governors, until age and education brought him reason and ability to govern himself and others? The necessities of his life, the health of his body, and the information of his mind would require him to be directed by the will of others and not his own; and yet will anyone think that this restraint and subjection were inconsistent with, or spoiled him of, that liberty or sovereignty he had a right to, or gave away his empire to those who had the government of his nonage? This government over him only prepared him the better and sooner for it. If anybody should ask me, when my son is *of age to be free?* I shall answer, just when his monarch is of age to govern. *But at what time,* says the judicious *Hooker,* Eccl. Pol. lib. i. sect. 6. *a man may be said to have attained so far forth the use of reason, as sufficeth to make him capable of those laws whereby he is then bound to guide his actions: this is a great deal more easy for sense to discern, than for any one by skill and learning to determine.*

§. 62. Commonwealths themselves take notice of and allow that there is a *time when men* are to *begin to act like free men,* and therefore until that time require not oaths of fealty or allegiance, or other public owning of, or submission to, the government of their countries.

§. 63. The *freedom* then of man and liberty of acting according to his own will is *grounded on* his having *reason,* which is able to instruct him in that law he is to govern himself by and make him know how far he is left to the freedom of his own will. To turn him loose to an unrestrained liberty before he has reason to guide him is not to allow him the privilege of his nature to be free, but to thrust him out amongst brutes and abandon him to a state as wretched, and as much beneath that of a man, as theirs. This is that which puts the *authority* into the *parents'* hands to govern the *minority* of their children. God hath made it their business to employ this care on their offspring and hath placed in them suitable inclinations of tenderness and concern to temper this power, to apply it as his wisdom designed it, to the children's good, as long as they should need to be under it.

§. 64. But what reason can hence advance this care of the *parents* due to their offspring into an *absolute arbitrary dominion* of the father, whose power reaches no farther than by such a discipline as he finds most effectual to give such strength and health to their bodies, such vigour and rectitude to their minds, as may best fit his children to be most useful to themselves and others, and, if it be necessary to his condition, to make them work, when they are able, for their own subsistence. But in this power the *mother* too has her share with the *father.*

§. 65. Nay, this *power* so little belongs to the *father* by any peculiar right of nature, but only as he is guardian of his children, that when he quits his care of them he loses his power over them, which goes along with their nourishment and education, to which it is inseparably annexed. And it belongs as much to the *foster-father* of an exposed child as to the natural father of another, so little power does the bare *act of begetting* give a man over his issue, if all his care ends there and this be all the title he hath to the name and authority of a father. And what will become of this *paternal power* in that part of the world where one woman hath more than one husband at a time, or in those parts of *America* where, when the husband and wife part, which happens frequently, the children are all left to the mother, follow her, and are wholly under her care and provision? If the father die whilst the children are young, do they not naturally everywhere owe the same obedience to their *mother*, during their minority, as to their father were he alive? And will anyone say that the mother hath a legislative power over her children, that she can make standing rules, which shall be of perpetual obligation, by which they ought to regulate all the concerns of their property and bound their liberty all the course of their lives? Or can she enforce the observation of them with capital punishments? For this is the proper *power of the magistrate*, of which the father hath not so much as the shadow. His command over his children is but temporary and reaches not their life or property. It is but a help to the weakness and imperfection of their nonage, a discipline necessary to their education; and though a *father* may dispose of his own possessions as he pleases, when his children are out of danger of perishing for want, yet *his power* extends not to the lives or goods which either their own industry or another's bounty has made theirs, nor to their liberty neither, when they are once arrived to the enfranchisement of the years of discretion. The *father's empire* then ceases, and he can from thence forwards no more dispose of the liberty of his son than

that of any other man; and it must be far from an absolute or perpetual jurisdiction from which a man may
withdraw himself, having licence from divine authority
to *leave father and mother and cleave to his wife.*

§. 66. But though there be a time when a *child* comes to
be as *free* from subjection to the will and command of his
father as the father himself is free from subjection to the
will of anybody else, and they are each under no other
restraint but that which is common to them both,
whether it be the law of nature or municipal law of their
country, yet this freedom exempts not a son from that
honour which he ought, by the law of God and nature, *to*
pay his *parents.* God having made the parents instru-
ments in his great design of continuing the race of mankind and the occasions of life to their children, as he hath
laid on them an obligation to nourish, preserve, and
bring up their offspring, so he has laid on the children a
perpetual obligation of *honouring their parents,* which
containing in it an inward esteem and reverence to be
shown by all outward expressions, ties up the child from
anything that may ever injure or affront, disturb or
endanger, the happiness or life of those from whom he
received his. And it engages him in all actions of defence,
relief, assistance and comfort of those by whose means he
entered into being and has been made capable of any
enjoyments of life. From this obligation no state, no freedom, can absolve children. But this is very far from giving parents a power of command over their children or
an authority to make laws and dispose as they please of
their lives or liberties. It is one thing to owe honour,
respect, gratitude and assistance, another to require an
absolute obedience and submission. The *honour due to
parents* a monarch in his throne owes his mother; and yet
this lessens not his authority nor subjects him to her
government.

§. 67. The subjection of a minor places in the father a temporary government which terminates with the minority of the child; and the *honour due from a child* places in the parents a perpetual right to respect, reverence, support and compliance too, more or less, as the father's care, cost, and kindness in his education has been more or less.° This ends not with minority, but holds in all parts and conditions of a man's life. The want of distinguishing these two powers, *viz.* that which the father hath in the right of *tuition,* during minority, and the right of *honour* all his life, may perhaps have caused a great part of the mistakes about this matter. For to speak properly of them, the first of these is rather the privilege of children and duty of parents than any prerogative of paternal power. The nourishment and education of their children is a charge so incumbent on parents for their children's good that nothing can absolve them from taking care of it. And though the *power of commanding and chastising* them go along with it, yet God hath woven into the principles of human nature such a tenderness for their offspring that there is little fear that parents should use their power with too much rigour. The excess is seldom on the severe side, the strong bias of nature drawing the other way. And therefore God almighty, when he would express his gentle dealing with the *Israelites,* he tells them that though he chastened them, *he chastened them as a man chastens his son,* Deut. viii. 5. *i. e.* with tenderness and affection, and kept them under no severer discipline than what was absolutely best for them and had been less kindness to have slackened. This is that power to which *children* are commanded *obedience,* that the pains and care of their parents may not be increased or ill rewarded.

§. 68. On the other side, *honour* and *support,* all that which gratitude requires to return for the benefits received by and from them, is the indispensable duty of the child and the proper privilege of the parents. This is intended for the parents' advantage, as the other is for the child's; though education, the parents' duty, seems to have most power because the ignorance and infirmities of childhood stand in need of restraint and correction, which is a visible exercise of rule and a kind of dominion. And that duty which is comprehended in the word *honour* requires less obedience, though the obligation be stronger on grown than younger children. For who can think the command, *Children obey your parents,* requires in a man that has children of his own the same submission to his father as it does in his yet young children to him, and that by this precept he were bound to obey all his father's commands, if, out of a conceit of authority, he should have the indiscretion to treat him still as a boy?

§. 69. The first part then of *paternal power,* or rather duty, which is *education,* belongs so to the father that it terminates at a certain season; when the business of education is over, it ceases of itself, and is also alienable before. For a man may put the tuition of his son in other hands, and he that has made his son an *apprentice* to another has discharged him, during that time, of a great part of his obedience both to himself and to his mother. But all the *duty of honour,* the other part, remains never the less entire to them; nothing can cancel that. It is so inseparable from them both that the father's authority cannot dispossess the mother of this right, nor can any man discharge his son from *honouring* her that bore him. But both these are very far from a power to make laws and enforce them with penalties that may reach estate, liberty, limbs and life. The power of commanding ends with nonage; and though, after that, *honour* and respect, support and defence, and whatsoever gratitude can oblige a man to for the highest benefits he is naturally capable of, be always due from a son to his parents, yet all this puts no scepter into the father's hand, no sovereign power of commanding. He has no dominion over his son's property or actions, nor any right that his will should prescribe to his son's in all things; however it may become his son in many things, not very inconvenient to him and his family, to pay a deference to it.

§. 70. A man may owe *honour* and respect to an ancient or wise man, defence to his child or friend, relief and support to the distressed, and gratitude to a benefactor, to such a degree that all he has, all he can do, cannot sufficiently pay it. But all these give no authority, no right to anyone of making laws over him from whom they are owing. And it is plain all this is due not only to the bare title of father, not only because, as has been said, it is owing to the mother too, but because these obligations to parents, and the degrees of what is required of children, may be varied by the different care and kindness, trouble and expence which is often employed upon one child more than another.

§. 71. This shows the reason how it comes to pass that *parents in societies,* where they themselves are subjects, retain a *power over their children* and have as much right to their subjection as those who are in the state of nature, which could not possibly be if all political power were only paternal and that in truth they were one and the same thing. For then all paternal power being in the prince, the subject could naturally have none of it. But these two *powers, political* and *paternal,* are so perfectly distinct and separate, are built upon so different foundations and given to so different ends, that every subject that is a father has as much a paternal power over his children as the prince has over his. And every prince that has parents owes them as much filial duty and obedience as the meanest of his subjects do to theirs, and can therefore contain not any part or degree of that kind of dominion which a prince or magistrate has over his subject.

§. 72. Though the obligation on the parents to *bring up* their children, and the obligation on children to *honour* their parents, contain all the power on the one hand, and submission on the other, which are proper to this relation, yet there is *another power* ordinarily *in the father* whereby he has a tie on the obedience of his children, which though it be common to him with other men, yet the occasions of showing it almost constantly happening to fathers in their private families; and the instances of it elsewhere being rare and less taken notice of, it passes in the world for a part of *paternal jurisdiction.* And this is the power men generally have to *bestow their estates* on those who please them best, the possession of the father being the expectation and inheritance of the children, ordinarily in certain proportions, according to the law and custom of each country. Yet it is commonly in the father's power to bestow it with a more sparing or liberal hand, according as the behaviour of this or that child hath comported with his will and humour.

§. 73. This is no small tie on the obedience of children. And there being always annexed to the enjoyment of land a submission to the government of the country of which that land is a part, it has been commonly supposed that a *father* could *oblige his posterity to that government* of which he himself was a subject, and that his compact held them; whereas, it being only a necessary condition annexed to the land and the inheritance of an estate which is under that government, reaches only those who will take it on that condition and so is no natural tie or engagement, but a voluntary submission. For *every man's children,* being by nature as *free* as himself or any of his ancestors ever were, may, whilst they are in that freedom, choose what society they will join themselves to, what commonwealth they will put themselves under.° But if they will enjoy the *inheritance* of their ancestors, they must take it on the same terms their ancestors had it and submit to all the conditions annexed to such a possession. By this power indeed fathers oblige their children to obedience to themselves, even when they are past minority, and most commonly too subject them to this or that political power. But neither of these by any peculiar right of *fatherhood,* but by the reward they have in their hands to enforce and recompence such a compliance, and is no more power than what a *French man* has over an *English man,* who by the hopes of an estate he will leave him will certainly have a strong tie on his obedience. And if, when it is left him he will enjoy it, he must certainly take it upon the conditions annexed to the *possession of land* in that country where it lies, whether it be *France* or *England.*

§. 74. To conclude then, though the *father's power* of commanding extends no farther than the minority of his children and to a degree only fit for the discipline and government of that age, and though that *honour* and *respect* and all that which the *Latins* called *piety,* which they indispensably owe to their parents all their lifetime and in all estates, with all that support and defence which is due to them, gives the father no power of governing, *i. e.* making laws and enacting penalties on his children; though by all this he has no dominion over the property or actions of his son, yet it is obvious to conceive how easy it was, in the first ages of the world and in places still, where the thinness of people gives families leave to separate into unpossessed quarters and they have room to remove or plant themselves in yet vacant habitations, for the *father of the family* to become the prince of it.[1] He had been a ruler from the beginning of the infancy of his children. And since without some government it would be hard for them to live together, it was likeliest it should, by the express or tacit consent of the children when they were grown up, be in the father, where it seemed without any change barely to continue; when indeed nothing more was required to it than permitting the *father* to exercise alone, in his family, that executive power of the law of nature which every free man naturally hath, and by that permission resigning up to him a monarchical power whilst they remained in it. But that this was not by any *paternal right,* but only by the consent of his children, is evident from hence: that nobody doubts but if a stranger, whom chance or business had brought to his family, had there killed any of his children or committed any other act, he might condemn and put him to death, or otherwise have punished him, as well as any of his children, which it was impossible he should do by virtue of any paternal authority over one who was not his child, but by virtue of that executive power of the law of nature, which, as a man, he had a right to. And he alone could punish him in his family, where the respect of his

1. It is no improbable opinion therefore, which the archphilosopher was of, that the chief person in every household was always, as it were, a king: so when numbers of households joined themselves in civil societies together, kings were the first kind of governors amongst them, which is also, as it seemeth, the reason why the name of fathers continued still in them, who, of fathers, were made rulers; as also the ancient custom of governors to do as *Melchizedec,* and being kings, to exercise the office of priests, which fathers did at the first, grew perhaps by the same occasion. Howbeit, this is not the only kind of regiment that has been received in the world. The inconveniences of one kind have caused sundry others to be devised; so that in a word, all public regiment, of what kind soever, seemeth evidently to have risen from the deliberate advice, consultation and composition between men, judging it convenient and behoveful; there being no impossibility in nature considered by itself, but that man might have lived without: any public regiment, *Hooker's Eccl. P. lib.* i. *sect.* 10.

children had laid by the exercise of such a power, to give way to the dignity and authority they were willing should remain in him, above the rest of his family.

§. 75. Thus it was easy and almost natural for children, by a tacit and scarce avoidable consent, to make way for the *father's authority and government.* They had been accustomed in their childhood to follow his direction and to refer their little differences to him; and when they were men, who fitter to rule them? Their little properties and less covetousness seldom afforded greater controversies; and when any should arise, where could they have a fitter umpire than he, by whose care they had everyone been sustained and brought up, and who had a tenderness for them all? It is no wonder that they made no distinction between minority and full age, nor looked after one and twenty or any other age that might make them the free disposers of themselves and fortunes, when they could have no desire to be out of their pupilage. The government they had been under during it continued still to be more their protection than restraint, and they could nowhere find a greater security to their peace, liberties, and fortunes than in the *rule of a father.*

§. 76. Thus the natural *fathers of families,* by an insensible change, became the *politic monarchs* of them too. And as they chanced to live long and leave able and worthy heirs for several successions or otherwise, so they laid the foundations of hereditary or elective kingdoms, under several constitutions and manners, according as chance, contrivance, or occasions happened to mould them. But if princes have their titles in their fathers' right, and it be a sufficient proof of the natural *right of fathers* to political authority because they commonly were those in whose hands we find, *de facto,* the exercise of government: I say, if this argument be good, it will as strongly prove that all princes, nay princes only, ought to be priests, since it is as certain that in the beginning *the father of the family was priest, as that he was ruler in his own household.*

CHAPTER VII

Of Political or Civil Society

§. 77. God having made man such a creature that, in his own judgment, it was not good for him to be alone, put him under strong obligations of necessity, convenience, and inclination to drive him into *society,* as well as fitted him with understanding and language to continue and enjoy it. The *first society* was between man and wife, which gave beginning to that between parents and children, to which, in time, that between master and servant came to be added. And though all these might, and commonly did, meet together and make up but one family, wherein the master or mistress of it had some sort of rule proper to a family, each of these, or all together, came short of *political society,* as we shall see if we consider the different ends, ties, and bounds of each of these.

§. 78. *Conjugal society* is made by a voluntary compact between man and woman.° And though it consist chiefly in such a communion and right in one another's bodies as is necessary to its chief end, procreation, yet it draws with it mutual support and assistance, and a communion of interests too, as necessary not only to unite their care and affection, but also necessary to their common off-spring, who have a right to be nourished and maintained by them until they are able to provide for themselves.

§. 79. For the end of *conjunction between male and female,* being not barely procreation, but the continuation of the species, this conjunction between male and female ought to last, even after procreation, so long as is necessary to the nourishment and support of the young ones, who are to be sustained by those that got them until they are able to shift and provide for themselves. This rule, which the infinite wise maker hath set to the works of his hands, we find the inferior creatures steadily obey. In those viviparous animals which feed on grass, the *conjunction between male and female* lasts no longer than the very act of copulation; because the teat of the dam being sufficient to nourish the young until it be able to feed on grass, the male only begets, but concerns not himself for the female or young, to whose sustenance he can contribute noth-ing. But in beasts of prey the *conjunction* lasts longer, because the dam not being able well to subsist herself and nourish her numerous offspring by her own prey alone, a more laborious, as well as more dangerous way of living than by feeding on grass, the assistance of the male is necessary to the maintenance of their common family, which cannot subsist until they are able to prey for them-selves but by the joint care of male and female. The same is to be observed in all birds (except some domestic ones, where plenty of food excuses the cock from feeding and taking care of the young brood), whose young needing food in the nest, the cock and hen continue mates until the young are able to use their wing and provide for themselves.

§. 80. And herein I think lies the chief, if not the only, reason *why the male and female in mankind are tied to a longer conjunction* than other creatures, *viz.* because the female is capable of conceiving, and *de facto* is commonly with child again and brings forth too a new birth, long before the former is out of a dependency for support on his parents' help and able to shift for himself, and has all the assistance is due to him from his parents. Whereby the father, who is bound to take care for those he hath begot, is under an obligation to continue in conjugal society with the same woman longer than other creatures, whose young being able to subsist of themselves before the time of procreation returns again, the conjugal bond dissolves of itself, and they are at liberty until *Hymen* at his usual anniversary season summons them again to choose new mates. Wherein one cannot but admire the wisdom of the great Creator who, having given to man foresight and an ability to lay up for the future, as well as to supply the present necessity, hath made it necessary that *society of man and wife should be more lasting* than of male and female amongst other creatures; that so their industry might be encouraged and their interest better united, to make provision and lay up goods for their common issue, which uncertain mixture or easy and frequent solutions of conjugal society would mightily disturb.

§. 81. But though these are ties upon *mankind* which make the *conjugal bonds* more firm and lasting in man than the other species of animals, yet it would give one reason to enquire why this *compact,* where procreation and education are secured and inheritance taken care for, may not be made determinable, either by consent, or at a certain time, or upon certain conditions, as well as any other voluntary compacts, there being no necessity in the nature of the thing nor to the ends of it that it should always be for life; I mean to such as are under no restraint of any positive law, which ordains all such contracts to be perpetual.

§. 82. But the husband and wife, though they have but one common concern, yet having different understandings will unavoidably sometimes have different wills too. It therefore being necessary that the last determination, *i. e.* the rule, should be placed somewhere, it naturally falls to the man's share, as the abler and the stronger.° But this reaching but to the things of their common interest and property leaves the wife in the full and free possession of what by contract is her peculiar right, and gives the husband no more power over her life than she has over his. The *power of the husband* being so far from that of an absolute monarch that the *wife* has in many cases a liberty to separate from him, where natural right or their contract allows it, whether that contract be made by themselves in the state of nature or by the customs or laws of the country they live in. And the children upon such separation fall to the father's or mother's lot, as such contract does determine.

§. 83. For all the ends of *marriage* being to be obtained under politic government, as well as in the state of nature, the civil magistrate doth not abridge the right or power of either naturally necessary to those ends, *viz.* procreation and mutual support and assistance whilst they are together, but only decides any controversy that may arise between man and wife about them. If it were otherwise, and that absolute *sovereignty* and power of life and death naturally belonged to the husband and were *necessary to the society between man and wife,* there could be no matrimony in any of those countries where the husband is allowed no such absolute authority. But the ends of matrimony requiring no such power in the husband, the condition of *conjugal society* put it not in him, it being not at all necessary to that state. *Conjugal society* could subsist and attain its ends without it; nay, community of goods, and the power over them, mutual assistance and maintenance, and other things belonging to *conjugal society* might be varied and regulated by that contract which unites man and wife in that society, as far as may consist with procreation and the bringing up of children until they could shift for themselves, nothing being necessary to any society that is not necessary to the ends for which it is made.

§. 84. The *society between parents and children,* and the distinct rights and powers belonging respectively to them, I have treated of so largely in the foregoing chapter, that I shall not here need to say anything of it. And I think it is plain that it is far different from a politic society.

§. 85. *Master* and *servant* are names as old as history, but given to those of far different condition. For a freeman makes himself a servant to another by selling him, for a certain time, the service he undertakes to do in exchange for wages he is to receive. And though this commonly puts him into the family of his master and under the ordinary discipline thereof, yet it gives the master but a temporary power over him and no greater than what is contained in the *contract* between them. But there is another sort of servants, which by a peculiar name we call *slaves,* who, being captives taken in a just war, are by the right of nature subjected to the absolute dominion and arbitrary power of their masters.° These men having, as I say, forfeited their lives, and with it their liberties, and lost their estates, and being in the *state of slavery* not capable of any property, cannot in that state be considered as any part of *civil society,* the chief end whereof is the preservation of property.

§. 86. Let us therefore consider a *master of a family* with all these subordinate relations of *wife, children, servants,* and *slaves* united under the domestic rule of a family, which, what resemblance soever it may have in its order, offices, and number too, with a little commonwealth, yet is very far from it, both in its constitution, power and end. Or if it must be thought a monarchy and the *paterfamilias* the absolute monarch in it, absolute monarchy will have but a very shattered and short power, when it is plain, by what has been said before, that the *master of the family* has a very distinct and differently limited *power,* both as to time and extent, over those several persons that are in it. For excepting the slave (and the family is as much a family, and his power as *paterfamilias* as great, whether there be any slaves in his family or no), he has no legislative power of life and death over any of them, and none too but what a *mistress of a family* may have as well as he. And he certainly can have no absolute power over the whole *family,* who has but a very limited one over every individual in it. But how a *family,* or any other society of men, differ from that which is properly *political society,* we shall best see by considering wherein *political society* itself consists.

§. 87. Man being born, as has been proved, with a title to perfect freedom and an uncontrolled enjoyment of all the rights and privileges of the law of nature, equally with any other man or number of men in the world, hath by nature a power not only to preserve his property, that is, his life, liberty and estate, against the injuries and attempts of other men, but to judge of and punish the breaches of that law in others, as he is persuaded the offence deserves, even with death itself in crimes where the heinousness of the fact, in his opinion, requires it. But because no *political society* can be nor subsist without having in itself the power to preserve the property, and in order thereunto, punish the offences of all those of that society, there, and there only is *political society,* where every one of the members hath quitted this natural power, resigned it up into the hands of the community in all cases that exclude him not from appealing for protection to the law established by it. And thus all private judgment of every particular member being excluded, the community comes to be umpire by settled standing rules, indifferent and the same to all parties, and by men having authority from the community for the execution of those rules, decides all the differences that may happen between any members of that society concerning any matter of right and punishes those offences which any member hath committed against the society with such penalties as the law has established. Whereby it is easy to discern who are and who are not in *political society* together. Those who are united into one body and have a common established law and judicature to appeal to, with authority to decide controversies between them and punish offenders, are in *civil society* one with another; but those who have no such common appeal, I mean on earth, are still in the state of nature, each being, where there is no other, judge for himself and executioner, which is, as I have before showed it, the perfect *state of nature.*

§. 88. And thus the commonwealth comes by a power to set down what punishment shall belong to the several transgressions which they think worthy of it, committed amongst the members of that society (which is the *power of making laws),* as well as it has the power to punish any injury done to any of its members by any one that is not of it (which is the *power of war and peace*), and all this for the preservation of the property of all the members of that society, as far as is possible. But though every man who has entered into civil society and is become a member of any commonwealth has thereby quitted his power to punish offences against the law of *nature,* in prosecution of his own private judgment, yet with the judgment of offences, which he has given up to the legislative in all cases where he can appeal to the magistrate, he has given a right to the commonwealth to employ his force for the execution of the judgments of the commonwealth whenever he shall be called to it, which indeed are his own judgments, they being made by himself or his representative. And herein we have the original of the *legislative* and *executive power* of civil society, which is to judge by standing laws how far offences are to be punished when committed within the commonwealth, and also to determine, by occasional judgments founded on the present circumstances of the fact, how far injuries from without are to be vindicated, and in both these to employ all the force of all the members when there shall be need.

§. 89. Wherever therefore any number of men are so united into one society as to quit everyone his executive power of the law of nature and to resign it to the public, there and there only is a *political or civil society.* And this is done wherever any number of men in the state of nature enter into society to make one people, one body politic, under one supreme government, or else when anyone joins himself to and incorporates with any government already made. For hereby he authorizes the society or, which is all one, the legislative thereof, to make laws for him as the public good of the society shall require, to the execution whereof his own assistance (as to his own decrees) is due. And this *puts men* out of a state of nature *into* that of a *commonwealth,* by setting up a judge on earth with authority to determine all the controversies and redress the injuries that may happen to any member of the commonwealth, which judge is the legislative or magistrates appointed by it. And wherever there are any number of men, however associated, that have no such decisive power to appeal to, there they are still in *the state of nature*.

§. 90. Hence it is evident that *absolute monarchy,* which by some men is counted the only government in the world, is indeed *inconsistent with civil society* and so can be no form of civil government at all. For the *end of civil society* being to avoid and remedy those inconveniencies of the state of nature which necessarily follow from every man's being judge in his own case, by setting up a known authority to which every one of that society may appeal upon any injury received or controversy that may arise and which every one of the society[1] ought to obey, wherever any persons are who have not such an authority to appeal to for the decision of any difference between them, there those persons are still *in the state of nature.* And so is every *absolute prince,* in respect of those who are under his *dominion*.

§. 91. For he being supposed to have all, both legislative and executive power, in himself alone, there is no judge to be found, no appeal lies open to anyone, who may fairly and indifferently and with authority decide, and from whose decision relief and redress may be expected of any injury or inconvenience that may be suffered from the prince or by his order, so that such a man, however titled, *Czar,* or *Grand Seignior,* or how you please, is as much *in the state of nature* with all under his dominion as he is with the rest of mankind. For wherever any two men are who have no standing rule and common judge

1. The public power of all society is above every soul contained in the same society; and the principal use of that power is, to give laws unto all that are under it, which laws in such cases we must obey, unless there be reason shewed which may necessarily inforce, that the law of reason, or of God, doth enjoin the contrary, *Hook. Eccl. Pol. l.* i. *sect.* 16.

to appeal to on earth for the determination of controversies of right between them, there they are still *in the state of nature*[2] and under all the inconveniencies of it, with only this woeful difference to the subject, or rather slave, of an absolute prince: that whereas in the ordinary state of nature he has a liberty to judge of his right and, according to the best of his power, to maintain it, now whenever his property is invaded by the will and order of his monarch, he has not only no appeal, as those in society ought to have, but, as if he were degraded from the common state of rational creatures, is denied a liberty to judge of or to defend his right, and so is exposed to all the misery and inconveniencies that a man can fear from one who, being in the unrestrained state of nature, is yet corrupted with flattery and armed with power.

§. 92. For he that thinks *absolute power purifies men's blood* and corrects the baseness of human nature need read but the history of this, or any other, age to be convinced of the contrary. He that would have been insolent and injurious in the woods of *America* would not probably be much better in a throne, where perhaps learning

2. To take away all such mutual grievances, injuries and wrongs, *i. e.* such as attend men in the state of nature, there was no way but only by growing into composition and agreement amongst themselves, by ordaining some kind of government public, and by yielding themselves subject thereunto, that unto whom they granted authority to rule and govern, by them the peace, tranquility and happy estate of the rest might be procured. Men always knew that where force and injury was offered, they might be defenders of themselves; they knew that however men may seek their own commodity, yet if this were done with injury unto others, it was not to be suffered, but by all men, and all good means to be withstood. Finally, they knew that no man might in reason take upon him to determine his own right, and according to his own determination proceed in maintenance thereof, in as much as every man is towards himself, and them whom he greatly affects, partial; and therefore that strifes and troubles would be endless, except they gave their common consent, all to be ordered by some, whom they should agree upon, without which consent there would be no reason that one man should take upon him to be lord or judge over another, *Hooker's Eccl. Pol. l.* i. *sect.* 10.

and religion shall be found out to justify all that he shall do to his subjects and the sword presently silence all those that dare question it. For what the *protection of absolute monarchy* is, what kind of fathers of their countries it makes princes to be, and to what a degree of happiness and security it carries civil society where this sort of government is grown to perfection, he that will look into the late relation of *Ceylon* may easily see.

§. 93. In *absolute monarchies* indeed, as well as other governments of the world, the subjects have an appeal to the law and judges to decide any controversies and restrain any violence that may happen between the subjects themselves, one amongst another. This everyone thinks necessary and believes he deserves to be thought a declared enemy to society and mankind who should go about to take it away. But whether this be from a true love of mankind and society and such a charity as we owe all one to another, there is reason to doubt. For this is no more than what every man who loves his own power, profit, or greatness may and naturally must do: keep those animals from hurting or destroying one another who labour and drudge only for his pleasure and advantage, and so are taken care of not out of any love the master has for them, but love of himself and the profit they bring him. For if it be asked what security, *what fence* is there in such a state *against the violence and oppression of this absolute ruler,* the very question can scarce be borne. They are ready to tell you that it deserves death only to ask after safety. Between subject and subject, they will grant, there must be measures, laws and judges, for their mutual peace and security; but as for the *ruler,* he ought to be *absolute* and is above all such circumstances. Because he has power to do more hurt and wrong, it is right when he does it. To ask how you may be guarded from harm or injury on that side where the strongest hand is to do it, is presently the voice of faction and rebellion, as if when men quitting the state of nature entered into society, they agreed that all of them but one should be under the restraint of laws, but that he should still retain all the liberty of the state of nature, increased with power and made licentious by impunity. This is to think that men are so foolish that they take care to avoid what mischiefs may be done them by *polecats* or *foxes*, but are content, nay, think it safety, to be devoured by *lions*.

§. 94. But whatever flatterers may talk to amuse peoples' understandings, it hinders not men from feeling. And when they perceive that any man, in what station soever, is out of the bounds of the civil society which they are of and that they have no appeal on earth against any harm they may receive from him, they are apt to think themselves in the state of nature in respect of him whom they find to be so, and to take care, as soon as they can, to have that *safety and security in civil society* for which it was first instituted and for which only they entered into it. And therefore, though perhaps at first (as shall be showed more at large hereafter in the following part of this discourse) some one good and excellent man having got a pre-eminency among the rest, had this deference paid to his goodness and virtue as to a kind of natural authority, that the chief rule with arbitration of their differences, by a tacit consent devolved into his hands, without any other caution but the assurance they had of his uprightness and wisdom; yet when time, giving authority and (as some men would persuade us) sacredness of customs, which the negligent and unforeseeing innocence of the first ages began, had brought in successors of another stamp, the people finding their properties not secure under the government as then it was (whereas government has no other end but the preservation of property[3]), could never be safe nor at rest, *nor think themselves in civil society,* until the legislature was placed in collective bodies of men, call them senate, parliament, or what you please. By which means every single person became subject, equally with other the meanest men, to those laws which he himself, as part of the legislative, had established. Nor could anyone, by his own authority, avoid the force of the law when once made, nor by any pretence of superiority plead exemption, thereby to license his own or the miscarriages of any of his dependents. *No man in civil society can be exempted from the laws of it.*[4] For if any man may do what he thinks fit, and there be no appeal on earth for redress or security against any harm he shall do, I ask whether he be not perfectly still in the state of nature and so can be *no part or member of that civil society,* unless anyone will say the state of nature and civil society are one and the same thing, which I have never yet found anyone so great a patron of anarchy as to affirm.

3. At the first, when some certain kind of regiment was once appointed, it may be that nothing was then farther thought upon for the manner of governing, but all permitted unto their wisdom and discretion, which were to rule, until by experience they found this for all parts very inconvenient, so as the thing which they had devised for a remedy, did indeed but increase the sore, which it should have cured. They saw, that *to live by one man's will, became the cause of all men's misery.* This constrained them to come unto laws, wherein all men might see their duty beforehand, and know the penalties of transgressing them. *Hooker's Eccl. Pol. l. i. sect.* 10.

4. Civil law being the act of the whole body politic, doth therefore over-rule each several part of the same body. *Hooker ibid.*

CHAPTER VIII

Of the Beginning of Political Societies

§. 95. Men being, as has been said, by nature all free, equal, and independent, no one can be put out of this estate and subjected to the political power of another without his own consent. The only way whereby any one divests himself of his natural liberty and puts on the *bonds of civil society* is by agreeing with other men to join and unite into a community, for their comfortable, safe, and peaceable living one amongst another, in a secure enjoyment of their properties and a greater security against any that are not of it. This any number of men may do, because it injures not the freedom of the rest; they are left as they were in the liberty of the state of nature. When any number of men have so *consented to make one community or government,* they are thereby presently incorporated and make *one body politic,* wherein the *majority* have a right to act and conclude the rest.

§. 96. For when any number of men have, by the consent of every individual, made a *community,* they have thereby made that *community* one body, with a power to act as one body, which is only by the will and determination of the *majority.* For that which acts any community, being only the consent of the individuals of it, and it being necessary to that which is one body to move one way, it is necessary the body should move that way whither the greater force carries it, which is the *consent of the majority.* Or else it is impossible it should act or continue one body, *one community,* which the consent of every individual that united into it agreed that it should. And so everyone is bound by that consent to be concluded by the *majority.*° And therefore we see that in assemblies, empowered to act by positive laws, where no number is set by that positive law which empowers them, the *act of the majority* passes for the act of the whole and of course determines, as having by the law of nature and reason, the power of the whole.

§. 97. And thus every man, by consenting with others to make one body politic under one government, puts himself under an obligation to everyone of that society to submit to the determination of the *majority* and to be concluded by it, or else this *original compact,* whereby he with others incorporates into *one society,* would signify nothing and be no compact, if he be left free and under no other ties than he was in before in the state of nature. For what appearance would there be of any compact, what new engagement if he were no farther tied by any decrees of the society than he himself thought fit and did actually consent to? This would be still as great a liberty as he himself had before his compact, or anyone else in the state of nature hath, who may submit himself and consent to any acts of it if he thinks fit.

§. 98. For if *the consent of the majority* shall not, in reason, be received as *the act of the whole* and conclude every individual, nothing but the consent of every individual can make anything to be the act of the whole. But such a consent is next to impossible ever to be had, if we consider the infirmities of health and avocations of business, which, in a number though much less than that of a commonwealth, will necessarily keep many away from the public assembly. To which if we add the variety of opinions and contrariety of interests which unavoidably happen in all collections of men, the coming into society upon such terms would be only like *Cato*'s coming into the theatre, only to go out again. Such a constitution as this would make the mighty *Leviathan* of a shorter duration than the feeblest creatures and not let it outlast the day it was born in, which cannot be supposed until we can think that rational creatures should desire and constitute societies only to be dissolved. For where the *majority* cannot conclude the rest, there they cannot act as one body and consequently will be immediately dissolved again.

§. 99. Whosoever therefore out of a state of nature unite into a *community* must be understood to give up all the power necessary to the ends for which they unite into society to the *majority* of the community, unless they expressly agreed in any number greater than the majority. And this is done by barely agreeing to *unite into one political society,* which is *all the compact* that is, or needs be, between the individuals that enter into or make up a *commonwealth.* And thus that which begins and actually *constitutes any political society* is nothing but the consent of any number of freemen capable of a majority to unite and incorporate into such a society. And this is that, and that only, which did or could give beginning to any *lawful government* in the world.

§. 100. To this I find two objections made:

First, *that there are no instances to be found in history of a company of men, independent and equal one amongst another, that met together and in this way began and set up a government.*

Second, *it is impossible of right that men should do so, because all men being born under government, they are to submit to that and are not at liberty to begin a new one.*°

§. 101. To the first there is this to answer: that it is not at all to be wondered that *history* gives us but a very little account of *men that lived together in the state of nature.* The inconveniencies of that condition and the love and want of society no sooner brought any number of them together, but they presently united and incorporated if they designed to continue together. And if we may not suppose *men* ever to have been *in the state of nature* because we hear not much of them in such a state, we may as well suppose the armies of *Salmanasser* or *Xerxes* were never children because we hear little of them until they were men and embodied in armies. Government is everywhere antecedent to records, and letters seldom come in amongst a people until a long continuation of civil society has, by other more necessary arts, provided for their safety, ease, and plenty; and then they begin to look after the history of their founders and search into their *original,* when they have outlived the memory of it. For it is with *commonwealths* as with particular persons: they are commonly *ignorant of their own births and infancies,* and if they know anything of their *original,* they are beholden for it to the accidental records that others have kept of it. And those that we have of the beginning of any polities in the world, excepting that of the *Jews,* where God himself immediately interposed and which favours not at all paternal dominion, are all either plain instances of such a beginning as I have mentioned or at least have manifest footsteps of it.

§. 102. He must show a strange inclination to deny evident matter of fact when it agrees not with his hypothesis, who will not allow that the *beginning* of *Rome* and *Venice* were by the uniting together of several men free and independent one of another, amongst whom there was no natural superiority or subjection. And if *Josephus Acosta*'s word may be taken, he tells us that in many parts of *America* there was no government at all. *There are great and apparent conjectures,* says he, *that these men,* speaking of those of Peru, *for a long time had neither kings nor commonwealths, but lived in troops, as they do this day in* Florida, *the* Cheriquanas, *those of* Brasil, *and many other nations, which have no certain kings, but as occasion is offered in peace or war they choose their captains as they please,* l. i. c. 25. If it be said that every man there was born subject to his father or the head of his family, that the subjection due from a child to a father took not away his freedom of uniting into what political society he thought fit has been already proved. But be that as it will, these men, it is evident, were actually *free;* and whatever superiority some politicians now would place in any of them, they themselves claimed it not, but by consent were all *equal,* until by the same consent they set rulers over themselves. So that their *politic societies* all *began* from a voluntary union and the mutual agreement of men freely acting in the choice of their governors and forms of government.

§. 103. And I hope those who went away from *Sparta* with *Palantus,* mentioned by *Justin,* l. iii. c. 4. will be allowed to have been *freemen independent* one of another and to have set up a government over themselves by their own consent. Thus I have given several examples, out of his-

tory, of *people free and in the state of nature*, that being
met together, incorporated and *began a commonwealth*.
And if the want of such instances be an argument to
prove that *government* were not nor could not be so
begun, I suppose the contenders for paternal empire were
better let it alone than urge it against natural liberty. For
if they can give so many instances out of history of *governments begun* upon paternal right, I think (though at
best an argument from what has been, to what should of
right be, has no great force) one might, without any great
danger, yield them the cause. But if I might advise them
in the case, they would do well not to search too much
into the *original of governments* as they have begun *de
facto*, lest they should find, at the foundation of most of
them, something very little favourable to the design they
promote and such a power as they contend for.

§. 104. But to conclude, reason being plain on our side
that men are naturally free, and the examples of history
showing that the *governments* of the world that were
begun in peace had their beginning laid on that foundation and were *made by the consent of the people*, there can
be little room for doubt either where the right is or what
has been the opinion or practice of mankind about the
first erecting of governments.

§. 105. I will not deny that if we look back as far as history
will direct us towards the *original of commonwealths*, we
shall generally find them under the government and
administration of one man.° And I am also apt to believe
that where a family was numerous enough to subsist by
itself and continued entire together, without mixing with
others, as it often happens where there is much land and
few people, the government commonly began in the
father. For the father, having by the law of nature the
same power with every man else to punish, as he thought

fit, any offences against that law, might thereby punish his transgressing children even when they were men and out of their pupilage. And they were very likely to submit to his punishment and all join with him against the offender, in their turns, giving him thereby power to execute his sentence against any transgression and so in effect make him the law-maker and governor over all that remained in conjunction with his family. He was fittest to be trusted, paternal affection secured their property and interest under his care, and the custom of obeying him, in their childhood, made it easier to submit to him, rather than to any other. If therefore they must have one to rule them, as government is hardly to be avoided amongst men that live together, who so likely to be the man as he that was their common father, unless negligence, cruelty, or any other defect of mind or body made him unfit for it? But when either the father died and left his next heir, for want of age, wisdom, courage, or any other qualities, less fit for rule, or where several families met and consented to continue together, there, it is not to be doubted, but they used their natural freedom to set up him whom they judged the ablest and most likely to rule well over them. Conformable hereunto we find the people of *America,* who (living out of the reach of the conquering swords and spreading domination of the two great empires of *Peru* and *Mexico)* enjoyed their own natural freedom, though, *cæteris paribus,* they commonly prefer the heir of their deceased king. Yet if they find him any way weak or incapable, they pass him by and set up the stoutest and bravest man for their ruler.

§. 106. Thus, though looking back as far as records give us any account of peopling the world and the history of nations, we commonly find the *government* to be in one hand, yet it destroys not that which I affirm, *viz.* that the *beginning of politic society* depends upon the consent of the individuals to join into and make one society, who, when they are thus incorporated, might set up what form of government they thought fit. But this having given occasion to men to mistake and think that by nature government was monarchical and belonged to the father, it may not be amiss here to consider why people in the beginning generally pitched upon this form: which, though perhaps the father's pre-eminency might in the first institution of some commonwealths give a rise to and place in the beginning the power in one hand, yet it is plain that the reason that continued the form of *government in a single person* was not any regard or respect to paternal authority, since all petty *monarchies,* that is, almost all monarchies, near their original have been commonly, at least upon occasion, *elective.*

§. 107. First then, in the beginning of things, the father's government of the childhood of those sprung from him, having accustomed them to the *rule of one man* and taught them that where it was exercised with care and skill, with affection and love to those under it, it was sufficient to procure and preserve to men all the political happiness they sought for in society, it was no wonder that they should pitch upon and naturally run into that form of government which from their infancy they had been all accustomed to and which, by experience, they had found both easy and safe. To which, if we add that *monarchy* being simple and most obvious to men whom neither experience had instructed in forms of government, nor the ambition or insolence of empire had taught to beware of the encroachments of prerogative or the inconveniencies of absolute power which monarchy in succession was apt to lay claim to and bring upon them, it was not at all strange that they should not much trouble themselves to think of methods of restraining any exorbitances of those to whom they had given the authority over them and of balancing the power of government by placing several parts of it in different hands. They had neither felt the oppression of tyrannical dominion, nor did the fashion of the age, nor their possessions, or way of living (which afforded little matter for covetousness or ambition) give them any reason to apprehend or provide against it. And therefore it is no wonder they put themselves into such a *frame of government* as was not only, as I said, most obvious and simple, but also best suited to their present state and condition, which stood more in need of defence against foreign invasions and injuries than of multiplicity of laws. The equality of a simple poor way of living, confining their desires within the narrow bounds of each man's small property, made few controversies and so no need of many laws to decide them or variety of officers to superintend the process or look after the execution of justice, where there were but few trespasses and few offenders. Since then those who liked one another so well as to join into society cannot but be supposed to have some acquaintance and friendship together and some trust one in another, they could not but have greater apprehensions of others than of one another. And therefore their first care and thought cannot but be supposed to be how to secure themselves against foreign force. It was natural for them to put themselves under a *frame of government* which might best serve to that end and choose the wisest and bravest man to conduct them in their wars and lead them out against their enemies, and in this chiefly be their *ruler.*

§. 108. Thus we see that the *kings* of the *Indians* in *America,* which is still a pattern of the first ages in *Asia* and *Europe,* whilst the inhabitants were too few for the country and want of people and money gave men no temptation to enlarge their possessions of land or contest for wider extent of ground, are little more than *generals of their armies.* And though they command absolutely in war, yet at home and in time of peace they exercise very little dominion and have but a very moderate sovereignty, the resolutions of peace and war being ordinarily either in the people or in a council, though the war itself, which admits not of plurality of governors, naturally devolves the command into the *king's sole authority.*

§. 109. And thus in *Israel* itself the *chief business of their judges and first kings* seems to have been *to be captains in war* and leaders of their armies, which (besides what is signified by *going out and in before the people*, which was to march forth to war and home again in the heads of their forces) appears plainly in the story of *Jephtha.* The *Ammonites* making war upon *Israel*, the *Gileadites* in fear send to *Jephtha*, a bastard of their family whom they had cast off, and article with him if he will assist them against the *Ammonites*, to make him their ruler; which they do in these words, *And the people made him head and captain over them*, Judg. xi. 11. which was, as it seems, all one as to be *judge. And he judged Israel*, Judg. xii. 7. that is, was their *captain-general six years.* So when *Jotham* upbraids the *Shechemites* with the obligation they had to *Gideon*, who had been their *judge* and ruler, he tells them, *He fought for you, and adventured his life far, and delivered you out of the hands of Midian*, Judg. ix. 17. Nothing is mentioned of him but what he did as a *general*, and indeed that is all that is found in his history or in any of the rest of the judges. And *Abimelech* particularly is called *king*, though at most he was but their *general.* And when, being weary of the ill conduct of *Samuel's* sons, the children of *Israel* desired a *king, like all the nations to judge them and to go out before them and to fight their battles*, 1 Sam. viii. 20. God granting their desire, says to *Samuel, I will send thee a man, and thou shalt anoint him to be captain over my people Israel, that he may save my people out of the hands of the Philistines,* ix. 16, as if the only *business of a king* had been to lead out their armies and fight in their defence, and accordingly at his inauguration pouring a vial of oil upon him, declares to *Saul* that *the Lord had anointed him to be captain over his inheritance,* x. 1. And therefore those, who after *Saul's* being solemnly chosen and saluted *king* by the *tribes* at *Mispah* were unwilling to have him their king, made no other objection but this, *How shall this man save us?* v. 27, as if they should have said, this man is unfit to be our *king,* not having skill and conduct enough in war to be able to defend us. And when God resolved to transfer the government to *David,* it is in these words, *But now thy kingdom shall not continue: the Lord hath sought him a man after his own heart, and the Lord hath commanded him to be captain over his people,* xiii. 14, as if the whole *kingly authority* were nothing else but to be their *general.* And therefore the *tribes* who had stuck to *Saul's* family and opposed *David's* reign, when they came to *Hebron* with terms of submission to him, they tell him, amongst other arguments they had to submit to him as to their king, that he was in effect their *king* in *Saul's* time, and therefore they had no reason but to receive him as their *king* now. *Also* (say they) *in time past, when Saul was king over us, thou wast he that leddest out and broughtest in Israel, and the Lord said unto thee, Thou shalt feed my people Israel, and thou shalt be a captain over Israel.*

§. 110. Thus, whether *a family* by degrees *grew up into a commonwealth* and the fatherly authority being continued on to the elder son, everyone in his turn growing up under it tacitly submitted to it, and the easiness and equality of it not offending anyone, every one acquiesced until time seemed to have confirmed it and settled a right of succession by prescription; or whether several families, or the descendants of several families, whom chance, neighbourhood, or business brought together, uniting into society, the need of a general whose conduct might defend them against their enemies in war, and the great confidence the innocence and sincerity of that poor but virtuous age (such as are almost all those which begin governments that ever come to last in the world) gave men one of another, made the first beginners of commonwealths generally put the rule into one man's hand, without any other express limitation or restraint but what the nature of the thing and the end of government required: whichever of those it was that at first put the rule into the hands of a single person, certain it is no body was entrusted with it but for the public good and safety, and to those ends, in the infancies of commonwealths, those who had it commonly used it. And unless they had done so, young societies could not have subsisted; without such nursing fathers, tender and careful of the public weal, all governments would have sunk under the weakness and infirmities of their infancy and the prince and the people had soon perished together.

§. 111. But though the *golden age*° (before vain ambition and *amor sceleratus habendi,* evil concupiscence, had corrupted men's minds into a mistake of true power and honour) had more virtue, and consequently better governors, as well as less vicious subjects; and there was then *no stretching prerogative,* on the one side, to oppress the people, *nor* consequently, on the other, any *dispute about privilege,* to lessen or restrain the power of the magistrate, and so no contest between rulers and people about governors or government: yet, when ambition and luxury in future ages would retain and increase the power[1] with-

---

1. At first, when some certain kind of regiment was once approved, it may be nothing was then farther thought upon for the manner of governing, but all

out doing the business for which it was given and, aided by flattery, taught princes to have distinct and separate interests from their people, men found it necessary to examine more carefully *the original* and rights *of government* and to find out ways to *restrain the exorbitances* and *prevent the abuses* of that power which, they having entrusted in another's hands only for their own good, they found was made use of to hurt them.

§. 112. Thus we may see how probable it is that people that were naturally free, and by their own consent either submitted to the government of their father or united together out of different families to make a government, should generally put the *rule into one man's hands* and choose to be under the conduct of a *single person,* without so much as by express conditions limiting or regulating his power, which they thought safe enough in his honesty and prudence, though they never dreamed of monarchy being *Jure Divino,* which we never heard of among mankind until it was revealed to us by the divinity of this last age, nor ever allowed paternal power to have a right to dominion or to be the foundation of all government. And thus much may suffice to show that as far as we have any light from history, we have reason to conclude that all peaceful beginnings of *government* have been *laid in the consent of the people.* I say *peaceful* because I shall have occasion in another place to speak of conquest, which some esteem a way of beginning of governments.

---

permitted unto their wisdom and discretion which were to rule, until by experience they found this for all parts very inconvenient, so as the thing which they had devised for a remedy, did indeed but increase the sore which it should have cured. They saw, that to live by one man's will, became the cause of all men's misery. This constrained them to come unto laws wherein all men might see their duty beforehand, and know the penalties of transgressing them. *Hooker's Eccl. Pol. l.* i. *sect.* 10.

The other objection I find urged against the beginning of polities, in the way I have mentioned, is this, viz.

§. 113. *That all men being born under government, some or other, it is impossible any of them should ever be free and at liberty to unite together and begin a new one or ever be able to erect a lawful government.*

If this argument be good, I ask how came so many lawful monarchies into the world? For if anybody, upon this supposition, can show me any one man in any age of the world *free* to begin a lawful monarchy, I will be bound to show him ten other *free men* at liberty, at the same time, to unite and begin a new government under a regal or any other form. It being demonstrable that if any one, *born under the dominion* of another, may be so *free* as to have a right to command others in a new and distinct empire, everyone that is *born under the dominion* of another may be so free too and may become a ruler or subject of a distinct separate government. And so by this their own principle, either all men, however *born,* are *free,* or else there is but one lawful prince, one lawful government in the world. And then they have nothing to do but barely to show us which that is, which when they have done, I doubt not but all mankind will easily agree to pay obedience to him.

§. 114. Though it be a sufficient answer to their objection to show that it involves them in the same difficulties that it doth those they use it against, yet I shall endeavour to discover the weakness of this argument a little farther.

All men, say they, *are born under government, and therefore they cannot be at liberty to begin a new one. Everyone is born a subject to his father, or his prince, and is therefore under the perpetual tie of subjection and allegiance.* It is plain mankind never owned nor considered any such natural *subjection that they were born in,* to one or to the other that tied them, without their own consents, to a subjection to them and their heirs.°

§. 115. For there are no examples so frequent in history, both sacred and profane, as those of men withdrawing themselves and their obedience from the jurisdiction they were born under and the family or community they were bred up in, and *setting up new governments* in other places. From whence sprang all that number of petty commonwealths in the beginning of ages, and which always multiplied as long as there was room enough, until the stronger or more fortunate swallowed the weaker, and those great ones again breaking to pieces, dissolved into lesser dominions. All which are so many testimonies against paternal sovereignty and plainly prove that it was not the natural right of the *father* descending to his heirs that made governments in the beginning, since it was impossible, upon that ground, there should have been so many little kingdoms. All must have been but only one universal monarchy, if men had not been at *liberty to separate* themselves from their families and the government, be it what it will, that was set up in it and go and make distinct commonwealths and other governments, as they thought fit.

§. 116. This has been the practice of the world from its first beginning to this day. Nor is it now any more hindrance to the freedom of mankind that they are *born under constituted and ancient polities* that have established laws and set forms of government, than if they were born in the woods, amongst the unconfined inhabitants that run loose in them. For those who would persuade us that *by being born under any government, we are naturally subjects to it* and have no more any title or pretense to the freedom of the state of nature, have no other reason (bating that of paternal power, which we have already answered) to produce for it, but only because our fathers or progenitors passed away their natural liberty and thereby bound up themselves and their posterity to a perpetual subjection to the government which they themselves submitted to. It is true that whatever engagements or promises anyone has made for himself, he is under the obligation of them, but *cannot,* by any *compact* whatsoever, *bind his children or posterity.* For his son, when a man, being altogether as free as the father, any *act of the father can no more give away the liberty of the son* than it can of anybody else. He may indeed annex such conditions to the land he enjoyed as a subject of any commonwealth as may oblige his son to be of that community if he will enjoy those possessions which were his father's, because that estate being his father's property, he may dispose or settle it as he pleases.

§. 117. And this has generally given the occasion to mistake in this matter, because commonwealths not permitting any part of their dominions to be dismembered nor to be enjoyed by any but those of their community, the son cannot ordinarily enjoy the possessions of his father but under the same terms his father did, by becoming a member of the society, whereby he puts himself presently under the government he finds there established, as much as any other subject of that commonwealth. And thus *the consent of freemen born under government,* which only *makes them members of it,* being given separately in their turns, as each comes to be of age, and not in a multitude together, people take no notice of it, and thinking it not done at all or not necessary, conclude they are naturally subjects as they are men.

§. 118. But, it is plain *governments* themselves understand it otherwise; they claim *no power over the son because of that they had over the father,* nor look on children as being their subjects by their fathers being so. If a subject of *England* have a child by an *English* woman in *France,* whose subject is he? Not the king of *England*'s, for he must have leave to be admitted to the privileges of it; nor the king of *France*'s, for how then has his father a liberty to bring him away and breed him as he pleases? And who ever was judged as a *traitor* or *deserter* if he left or warred against a country, for being barely born in it of parents that were aliens there? It is plain then, by the practice of governments themselves as well as by the law of right reason, that *a child is born a subject of no country or government.* He is under his father's tuition and authority until he comes to age of discretion; and then he is a freeman, at liberty what government he will put himself under, what body politic he will unite himself to. For if an *Englishman*'s son, born in *France,* be at liberty and may do so, it is evident there is no tie upon him by his father's being a subject of this kingdom; nor is he bound up by any compact of his ancestors. And why then hath not his son, by the same reason, the same liberty, though he be born anywhere else, since the power that a father hath naturally over his children is the same wherever they be born, and the ties of natural obligations are not bounded by the positive limits of kingdoms and commonwealths?

§. 119. *Every man* being, as has been showed, *naturally free,* and nothing being able to put him into subjection to any earthly power but only his own *consent,* it is to be considered what shall be understood to be a *sufficient declaration* of a man's *consent to make him subject* to the laws of any government. There is a common distinction of an express and a tacit consent which will concern our present case. Nobody doubts but an express *consent* of any man entering into any society makes him a perfect member of that society, a subject of that government. The difficulty is what ought to be looked upon as a *tacit con-*

sent and how far it binds, *i. e.* how far any one shall be looked on to have consented, and thereby submitted to any government, where he has made no expressions of it at all. And to this I say that every man that hath any possessions or enjoyment of any part of the dominions of any government, doth thereby give his *tacit consent* and is as far forth obliged to obedience to the laws of that government, during such enjoyment, as anyone under it, whether this his possession be of land, to him and his heirs forever, or a lodging only for a week, or whether it be barely travelling freely on the highway; and in effect, it reaches as far as the very being of any one within the territories of that government.°

§. 120. To understand this the better, it is fit to consider that every man, when he at first incorporates himself into any commonwealth, he, by his uniting himself thereunto, annexed also and submits to the community those possessions which he has or shall acquire that do not already belong to any other government. For it would be a direct contradiction for anyone to enter into society with others for the securing and regulating of property, and yet to suppose his land, whose property is to be regulated by the laws of the society, should be exempt from the jurisdiction of that government to which he himself, the proprietor of the land, is a subject. By the same act therefore whereby any one unites his person, which was before free, to any commonwealth, by the same he unites his possessions, which were before free, to it also; and they become, both of them, person and possession, subject to the government and dominion of that commonwealth, as long as it hath a being. Whoever therefore, from thenceforth, by inheritance, purchase, permission, or otherwise, *enjoys any part of the land* so annexed to and under the government *of that commonwealth, must take it with the condition* it is under: that is, *of submitting to the gov-*

ernment of the commonwealth under whose jurisdiction it is, as far forth as any subject of it.°

§. 121. But since the government has a direct jurisdiction only over the land and reaches the possessor of it (before he has actually incorporated himself in the society) only as he dwells upon and enjoys that, the obligation any one is under, by virtue of such enjoyment, to *submit to the government, begins and ends with the enjoyment;* so that whenever the owner, who has given nothing but such a *tacit consent* to the government, will by donation, sale, or otherwise quit the said possession, he is at liberty to go and incorporate himself into any other commonwealth, or to agree with others to begin a new one, *in vacuis locis,* in any part of the world they can find free and unpossessed. Whereas he that has once, by actual agreement and any *express* declaration, given his *consent* to be of any commonwealth, is perpetually and indispensably obliged to be and remain unalterably a subject to it, and can never be again in the liberty of the state of nature, unless, by any calamity, the government he was under comes to be dissolved, or else by some public act cuts him off from being any longer a member of it.

§. 122. But submitting to the laws of any country, living quietly and enjoying privileges and protection under them, *makes not a man a member of that society.* This is only a local protection and homage due to and from all those who, not being in a state of war, come within the territories belonging to any government, to all parts whereof the force of its laws extends. But this no more *makes a man a member of that society,* a perpetual subject of that commonwealth, than it would make a man a subject to another in whose family he found it convenient to abide for some time, though, whilst he continued in it, he were obliged to comply with the laws and submit to the government he found there. And thus we see that *foreigners,* by living all their lives under another government and enjoying the privileges and protection of it, though they are bound, even in conscience, to submit to its administration, as far forth as any denizen, yet do not thereby come to be *subjects or members of that commonwealth.* Nothing can make any man so but his actually entering into it by positive engagement and express promise and compact. This is that which I think concerning the beginning of political societies and that *consent which makes any one a member* of any commonwealth.°

CHAPTER IX

Of the Ends of Political Society
and Government

§. 123. If man in the state of nature be so free, as has been said, if he be absolute lord of his own person and possessions, equal to the greatest and subject to nobody, why will he part with his freedom? Why will he give up this empire and subject himself to the dominion and control of any other power? To which it is obvious to answer, that though in the state of nature he hath such a right, yet the enjoyment of it is very uncertain and constantly exposed to the invasion of others. For all being kings as much as he, every man his equal, and the greater part no strict observers of equity and justice, the enjoyment of the property he has in this state is very unsafe, very insecure. This makes him willing to quit a condition which, however free, is full of fears and continual dangers. And it is not without reason that he seeks out and is willing to join in society with others who are already united, or have a mind to unite, for the mutual *preservation* of their lives, liberties and estates, which I call by the general name, *property.*°

§. 124. The great and *chief end,* therefore, of men's uniting into commonwealths and putting themselves under government *is the preservation of their property.* To which in the state of nature there are many things wanting:

First, there wants an *established,* settled, known *law,* received and allowed by common consent to be the standard of right and wrong and the common measure to decide all controversies between them. For though the law of nature be plain and intelligible to all rational creatures, yet men being biased by their interest, as well as ignorant for want of study of it, are not apt to allow of it as a law binding to them in the application of it to their particular cases.

§. 125. *Secondly,* in the state of nature there wants *a known and indifferent judge* with authority to determine all differences according to the established law. For everyone in that state being both judge and executioner of the law of nature, men being partial to themselves, passion and revenge is very apt to carry them too far and with too much heat in their own cases, as well as negligence and unconcernedness to make them too remiss in other men's.

§. 126. *Thirdly,* in the state of nature there often wants *power* to back and support the sentence when right and to *give* it due *execution.* They who by any injustice offended will seldom fail, where they are able, by force to make good their injustice; such resistance many times makes the punishment dangerous, and frequently destructive, to those who attempt it.

§. 127. Thus mankind, notwithstanding all the privileges of the state of nature, being but in an ill condition while they remain in it, are quickly driven into society. Hence it comes to pass that we seldom find any number of men live any time together in this state. The inconveniencies that they are therein exposed to by the irregular and uncertain exercise of the power every man has of punishing the transgressions of others, make them take sanctuary under the established laws of government and therein seek *the preservation of their property*. It is this that makes them so willingly give up every one his single power of punishing, to be exercised by such alone as shall be appointed to it amongst them and by such rules as the community, or those authorized by them to that purpose, shall agree on. And in this we have the original *right and rise of both the legislative and executive power,* as well as of the governments and societies themselves.

§. 128. For in the state of nature, to omit the liberty he has of innocent delights, a man has two powers.

The first is to do whatsoever he thinks fit for the preservation of himself and others within the permission of the *law of nature,* by which law, common to them all, he and all the rest of *mankind are one community,* make up one society, distinct from all other creatures. And were it not for the corruption and viciousness of degenerate men, there would be no need of any other, no necessity that men should separate from this great and natural community and by positive agreements combine into smaller and divided associations.

The other power a man has in the state of nature is the *power to punish the crimes* committed against that law. Both these he gives up when he joins in a private, if I may so call it, or particular politic society and incorporates into any commonwealth, separate from the rest of mankind.

§. 129. The first *power, viz. of doing whatsoever he thought fit for the preservation of himself* and the rest of mankind, *he gives up* to be regulated by laws made by the society, so far forth as the preservation of himself and the rest of that society shall require, which laws of the society in many things confine the liberty he had by the law of nature.

§. 130. *Secondly,* the *power of punishing he wholly gives up*° and engages his natural force (which he might before employ in the execution of the law of nature, by his own single authority, as he thought fit) to assist the executive power of the society, as the law thereof shall require. For being now in a new state, wherein he is to enjoy many conveniencies from the labour, assistance, and society of others in the same community, as well as protection from its whole strength, he is to part also with as much of his natural liberty in providing for himself as the good, prosperity, and safety of the society shall require, which is not only necessary, but just, since the other members of the society do the like.

§. 131. But though men, when they enter into society, give up the equality, liberty, and executive power they had in the state of nature into the hands of the society, to be so far disposed of by the legislative as the good of the society shall require, yet it being only with an intention in every-one the better to preserve himself, his liberty and property (for no rational creature can be supposed to change his condition with an intention to be worse), the power of the society or *legislative* constituted by them, can *never be supposed to extend farther than the common good,* but is obliged to secure every one's property, by providing against those three defects above mentioned that made the state of nature so unsafe and uneasy. And so whoever has the legislative or supreme power of any commonwealth is bound to govern by established *standing laws,* promulgated and known to the people, and not by extemporary decrees, by *indifferent* and upright *judges,* who are to decide controversies by those laws, and to employ the force of the community at home *only in the execution of such laws,* or abroad to prevent or redress foreign injuries and secure the community from inroads and invasion. And all this is to be directed to no other *end* but the *peace, safety,* and *public good* of the people.

CHAPTER X

Of the Forms of a Commonwealth

§. 132. The majority having, as has been showed, upon men's first uniting into society, the whole power of the community naturally in them, may employ all that power in making laws for the community from time to time and executing those laws by officers of their own appointing; and then the *form* of the government is a perfect *democracy*; or else may put the power of making laws into the hands of a few select men and their heirs or successors, and then it is an *oligarchy*; or else into the hands of one man, and then it is a *monarchy*, if to him and his heirs it is an *hereditary monarchy*, if to him only for life, but upon his death the power only of nominating a successor to return to them, an *elective monarchy*. And so accordingly of these the community may make compounded and mixed forms of government, as they think good. And if the legislative power be at first given by the majority to one or more persons only for their lives, or any limited time, and then the supreme power to revert to them again, when it is so reverted the community may dispose of it again anew into what hands they please and so constitute a new form of government. For the *form of government depending upon the placing the* supreme power, which is *the legislative,* it being impossible to conceive that an inferior power should prescribe to a superior, or any but the supreme make laws, according as the power of making laws is placed, such is the *form of the commonwealth.*°

§. 133. By *commonwealth* I must be understood all along to mean not a democracy, or any form of government, but *any independent community,* which the *Latines* signified by the word *civitas,* to which the word which best answers in our language is *commonwealth,* and most properly expresses such a society of men, which community or city in *English* does not. For there may be subordinate communities in a government, and city amongst us has a quite different notion from commonwealth. And therefore, to avoid ambiguity, I crave leave to use the word *commonwealth* in that sense in which I find it used by king *James the first.* And I take it to be its genuine signification, which if anybody dislike, I consent with him to change it for a better.°

CHAPTER XI

Of the Extent of the Legislative Power

§. 134. The great end of men's entering into society being the enjoyment of their properties in peace and safety, and the great instrument and means of that being the laws established in that society, the *first and fundamental positive law* of all commonwealths *is the establishing of the legislative* power; as the *first and fundamental natural law,* which is to govern even the legislative itself, *is the preservation of the society* and (as far as will consist with the public good) of every person in it. This *legislative* is not only *the supreme power* of the commonwealth, but sacred and unalterable in the hands where the community have once placed it. Nor can any edict of anybody else, in what form soever conceived, or by what power soever backed, have the force and obligation of a *law,* which has not its *sanction from* that *legislative* which the public has chosen and appointed. For without this the law could not have that which is absolutely necessary to its being a *law, the consent of the society*,[1] over whom nobody can have a power to make laws but by their own consent and by authority received from them. And therefore all the *obedience* which by the most solemn ties anyone can be obliged *to* pay ultimately terminates in this *supreme power* and is directed by those laws which it enacts. Nor can any oaths to any foreign power whatsoever, or any domestic subordinate power, discharge any member of the society from his *obedience to the legislative*, acting pursuant to their trust, nor oblige him to any obedience contrary to the laws so enacted or farther than they do allow, it being ridiculous to imagine one can be tied ultimately to *obey* any *power* in the society which is not the *supreme*.

§. 135. Though the *legislative*, whether placed in one or more, whether it be always in being or only by intervals, though it be the *supreme* power in every commonwealth, yet:

First, it is *not* nor can possibly be absolutely *arbitrary* over the lives and fortunes of the people. For it being but the joint power of every member of the society given up to that person or assembly which is legislator, it can be no

---

1. The lawful power of making laws to command whole politic societies of men, belonging so properly unto the same entire societies, that for any prince or potentate of what kind soever upon earth, to exercise the same of himself, and not by express commission immediately and personally received from God, or else by authority derived at the first from their consent, upon whose persons they impose laws, it is no better than mere tyranny. Laws they are not therefore which public approbation hath not made so. *Hooker's Eccl. Pol. l.* i. *sect.* 10. Of this point therefore we are to note, that sith men naturally have no full and perfect power to command whole politic multitudes of men, therefore utterly without our consent, we could in such sort be at no man's commandment living. And to be commanded we do consent, when that society, whereof we be a part, hath at any time before consented, without revoking the same after by the like universal agreement.

Laws therefore human, of what kind so ever, are available by consent. *Ibid.*

more than those persons had in a state of nature before they entered into society and gave up to the community. For nobody can transfer to another more power than he has in himself; and nobody has an absolute arbitrary power over himself, or over any other, to destroy his own life or take away the life or property of another. A man, as has been proved, cannot subject himself to the arbitrary power of another. And having in the state of nature no arbitrary power over the life, liberty, or possession of another, but only so much as the law of nature gave him for the preservation of himself and the rest of mankind, this is all he doth or can give up to the commonwealth, and by it to the *legislative power*, so that the legislative can have no more than this. Their power, in the utmost bounds of it, is *limited to the public good* of the society. It is a power that hath no other end but preservation and therefore can never have a right to destroy, enslave, or designedly to impoverish the subjects.[2] The obligations of the law of nature cease not in society, but only in many cases are drawn closer and have by human laws known penalties annexed to them to enforce their observation. Thus the law of nature stands as an eternal rule to all men, *legislators* as well as others.° The *rules* that they

2. Two foundations there are which bear up public societies; the one a natural inclination, whereby all men desire sociable life and fellowship; the other an order, expressly or secretly agreed upon, touching the manner of their union in living together: the latter is that which we call the law of a common-weal, the very soul of a politic body, the parts whereof are by law animated, held together, and set on work in such actions as the common good requireth. Laws politic, ordained for external order and regiment amongst men, are never framed as they should be, unless presuming the will of man to be inwardly obstinate, rebellious, and averse from all obedience to the sacred laws of his nature; in a word, unless presuming man to be, in regard of his depraved mind, little better than a wild beast, they do accordingly provide, notwithstanding, so to frame his outward actions, that they be no hindrance unto the common good, for which societies are instituted. Unless they do this, they are not perfect. *Hooker's Eccl. Pol. l.* i. *sect.* 10.

make for other men's actions must, as well as their own and other men's actions, be conformable to the law of nature, *i. e.* to the will of God, of which that is a declaration. And the *fundamental law of nature being the preservation of mankind,* no human sanction can be good or valid against it.

§. 136. *Secondly,* the *legislative,* or supreme authority, cannot assume to itself a power to rule by extemporary arbitrary decrees,[3] but *is bound to dispense justice* and decide the rights of the subject *by promulgated standing laws and known authorized judges.* For the law of nature being unwritten, and so nowhere to be found but in the minds of men, they who through passion or interest shall miscite or misapply it cannot so easily be convinced of their mistake where there is no established judge. And so it serves not, as it ought, to determine the rights and fence the properties of those that live under it, especially where everyone is judge, interpreter, and executioner of it too, and that in his own case. And he that has right on his side, having ordinarily but his own single strength, hath not force enough to defend himself from injuries or to punish delinquents. To avoid these inconveniencies which disorder men's properties in the state of nature, men unite into societies, that they may have the united strength of the whole society to secure and defend their properties and may have *standing rules* to bound it, by which everyone may know what is his. To this end it is that men give up all

---

3. Human laws are measures in respect of men whose actions they must direct, howbeit such measures they are as have also their higher rules to be measured by, which rules are two, the law of God, and the law of nature; so that laws human must be made according to the general laws of nature, and without contradiction to any positive law of scripture, otherwise they are ill made. *Hooker's Eccl. Pol. l.* iii. *sect.* 9.

To constrain men to anything inconvenient doth seem unreasonable. *Ibid. l.* i. *sect.* 10.

their natural power to the society which they enter into, and the community put the legislative power into such hands as they think fit, with this trust: that they shall be governed by *declared laws,* or else their peace, quiet, and property will still be at the same uncertainty as it was in the state of nature.

§. 137. Absolute arbitrary power, or governing without *settled standing laws,* can neither of them consist with the ends of society and government, which men would not quit the freedom of the state of nature for and tie themselves up under, were it not to preserve their lives, liberties and fortunes and by *stated rules* of right and property to secure their peace and quiet. It cannot be supposed that they should intend, had they a power so to do, to give to any one, or more, an *absolute arbitrary power* over their persons and estates and put a force into the magistrate's hand to execute his unlimited will arbitrarily upon them. This were to put themselves into a worse condition than the state of nature, wherein they had a liberty to defend their right against the injuries of others and were upon equal terms of force to maintain it, whether invaded by a single man or many in combination. Whereas by supposing they have given up themselves to the *absolute arbitrary power* and will of a legislator, they have disarmed themselves and armed him to make a prey of them when he pleases, he being in a much worse condition who is exposed to the arbitrary power of one man, who has the command of 100,000, than he that is exposed to the arbitrary power of 100,000 single men; nobody being secure that his will, who has such a command, is better than that of other men, though his force be 100,000 times stronger. And therefore, whatever form the commonwealth is under, the ruling power ought to govern by *declared* and *received laws,* and not by extemporary dictates and undetermined resolutions. For then mankind will be in a far worse condition than in the state of nature, if they shall have armed one or a few men with the joint power of a multitude, to force them to obey at pleasure the exorbitant and unlimited decrees of their sudden thoughts or unrestrained and until that moment unknown wills, without having any measures set down which may guide and justify their actions. For all the power the government has, being only for the good of the society, as it ought not to be *arbitrary* and at pleasure, so it ought to be exercised by *established and promulgated laws,* that both the people may know their duty and be safe and secure within the limits of the law; and the rulers too kept within their bounds, and not be tempted by the power they have in their hands, to employ it to such purposes and by such measures as they would not have known and own not willingly.

§. 138. *Thirdly,* the *supreme power cannot take* from any man any part of his *property* without his own consent.° For the preservation of property being the end of government and that for which men enter into society, it necessarily supposes and requires that the people should *have property,* without which they must be supposed to lose that, by entering into society, which was the end for which they entered into it: too gross an absurdity for any man to own. *Men* therefore *in society having property,* they have such a right to the goods which by the law of the community are theirs, that nobody hath a right to take their substance or any part of it from them without their own consent. Without this they have no *property* at all, for I have truly no *property* in that which another can by right take from me when he pleases, against my consent. Hence it is a mistake to think that the *supreme or legislative power* of any commonwealth can do what it will and dispose of the estates of the subject *arbitrarily* or take any part of them at pleasure. This is not much to be feared in governments where the *legislative* consists, wholly or in part, in assemblies which are variable, whose members, upon the dissolution of the assembly are subjects under the common laws of their country, equally with the rest. But in governments where the *legislative* is in one lasting assembly always in being or in one man, as in absolute monarchies, there is danger still that they will think themselves to have a distinct interest from the rest of the community, and so will be apt to increase their own riches and power by taking what they think fit from the people. For a man's *property* is not at all secure, though there be good and equitable laws to set the bounds of it between him and his fellow subjects, if he who commands those subjects have power to take from any private man what part he pleases of his *property* and use and dispose of it as he thinks good.

§. 139. But *government,* into whatsoever hands it is put, being, as I have before showed, entrusted with this condition and *for this end,* that men might have and secure their *properties,* the prince or senate, however it may have power to make laws for the regulating of *property* between the subjects one amongst another, yet can never have a power to take to themselves the whole or any part of the subjects' *property* without their own consent. For this would be in effect to leave them no *property* at all. And to let us see that even *absolute power,* where it is necessary, is *not arbitrary* by being absolute,° but is still limited by that reason and confined to those ends which required it in some cases to be absolute, we need look no farther than the common practice of martial discipline. For the preservation of the army, and in it of the whole commonwealth, requires an *absolute obedience* to the command of every superior officer, and it is justly death to disobey or dispute the most dangerous or unreasonable of them. But yet we see that neither the sergeant, that could command a soldier to march up to the mouth of a cannon or stand in a breach where he is almost sure to perish, can command that soldier to give him one penny of his money, nor the *general,* that can condemn him to death for deserting his post or for not obeying the most desperate orders, can yet, with all his *absolute power* of life and death, dispose of one farthing of that soldier's estate or seize one jot of his goods, whom yet he can command anything and hang for the least disobedience; because such a blind obedience is necessary to that end for which the commander has his power, *viz.* the preservation of the rest, but the disposing of his goods has nothing to do with it.

§. 140. It is true governments cannot be supported without great charge, and it is fit everyone who enjoys his share of the protection should pay out of his estate his proportion for the maintenance of it. But still it must be with his own consent, *i. e.* the consent of the majority, giving it either by themselves or their representatives chosen by them. For if any one shall claim a *power to lay* and levy *taxes* on the people by his own authority, and without such consent of the people, he thereby invades the *fundamental law of property* and subverts the end of government. For what property have I in that which another may by right take, when he pleases, to himself?

§. 141. *Fourthly,* the *legislative cannot transfer the power of making laws* to any other hands, for it being but a delegated power from the people, they who have it cannot pass it over to others. The people alone can appoint the form of the commonwealth, which is by constituting the legislative and appointing in whose hands that shall be. And when the people have said, 'we will submit to rules and be governed by *laws* made by such men and in such forms,' nobody else can say other men shall make *laws* for them. Nor can the people be bound by any *laws* but such as are enacted by those whom they have chosen and authorized to make *laws* for them. The power of the *legislative,* being derived from the people by a positive voluntary grant and institution, can be no other than what that positive grant conveyed, which being only to make *laws,* and not to make *legislators,* the *legislative* can have no power to transfer their authority of making laws and place it in other hands.

§. 142. These are the *bounds* which the trust that is put in them by the society, and the law of God and nature, have *set to the legislative* power of every commonwealth, in all forms of government.

First, they are to govern by *promulgated established laws,* not to be varied in particular cases, but to have one rule for rich and poor, for the favourite at court and the country man at plough.

Secondly, these *laws* also ought to be designed *for* no other end ultimately but *the good of the people.*

Thirdly, they must *not raise taxes* on the *property of the people without the consent of the people,* given by themselves or their deputies. And this properly concerns only such governments where the *legislative* is always in being, or at least where the people have not reserved any part of the legislative to deputies, to be from time to time chosen by themselves.

Fourthly, the *legislative* neither must *nor can transfer the power of making laws* to anybody else, or place it anywhere but where the people have.

CHAPTER XII

Of the Legislative, Executive, and Federative Power of the Commonwealth

§. 143. The *legislative* power is that which has a right *to direct how the force of the commonwealth* shall be employed for preserving the community and the members of it. But because those laws which are constantly to be executed and whose force is always to continue may be made in a little time, therefore there is no need that the *legislative* should be always in being, not having always business to do. And because it may be too great a temptation to human frailty, apt to grasp at power, for the same persons who have the power of making laws to have also in their hands the power to execute them, whereby they may exempt themselves from obedience to the laws they make and suit the law, both in its making and execution, to their own private advantage, and thereby come to have a distinct interest from the rest of the community, contrary to the end of society and government: therefore in well-ordered commonwealths, where the good of the whole is so considered, as it ought, the *legislative* power is put into the hands of divers persons who, duly assembled, have by themselves or jointly with others a power to make laws, which when they have done, being separated again, they are themselves subject to the laws they have made; which is a new and near tie upon them to take care that they make them for the public good.°

§. 144. But because the laws that are at once and in a short time made have a constant and lasting force and need a *perpetual execution* or an attendance thereunto, therefore it is necessary there should be a *power always in being* which should see to the *execution* of the laws that are made and remain in force. And thus the *legislative* and *executive power* come often to be separated.

§. 145. There is another *power* in every commonwealth which one may call *natural*, because it is that which answers to the power every man naturally had before he entered into society. For though in a commonwealth the members of it are distinct persons still in reference to one another, and as such are governed by the laws of the society, yet in reference to the rest of mankind they make one body, which is, as every member of it before was, still in the state of nature with the rest of mankind. Hence it is that the controversies that happen between any man of the society with those that are out of it are managed by the public, and an injury done to a member of their body engages the whole in the reparation of it. So that under this consideration, the whole community is one body in the state of nature in respect of all other states or persons out of its community.

§. 146. This therefore contains the power of war and peace, leagues and alliances, and all the transactions with all persons and communities without the commonwealth, and may be called *federative*,° if any one pleases. So the thing be understood, I am indifferent as to the name.

§. 147. These two powers, *executive* and *federative*, though they be really distinct in themselves, yet one comprehending the *execution* of the municipal laws of the society *within* itself upon all that are parts of it, the other the management of the *security and interest of the public without* with all those that it may receive benefit or damage from, yet they are always almost united. And though this *federative power*, in the well or ill management of it, be of great moment to the commonwealth, yet it is much less capable to be directed by antecedent, standing, positive laws than the *executive*, and so must necessarily be left to the prudence and wisdom of those whose hands it is in, to be managed for the public good. For the *laws* that concern subjects one amongst another, being to direct their actions, may well enough *precede* them. But what is to be done in reference to *foreigners*, depending much upon their actions and the variation of designs and interests, must be *left* in great part to the *prudence* of those who have this power committed to them, to be managed by the best of their skill for the advantage of the commonwealth.

§. 148. Though, as I said, the *executive* and *federative power* of every community be really distinct in themselves, yet they are hardly to be separated and placed at the same time in the hands of distinct persons. For both of them requiring the force of the society for their exercise, it is almost impracticable to place the force of the commonwealth in distinct and not subordinate hands, or that the *executive* and *federative power* should be *placed* in persons that might act separately, whereby the force of the public would be under different commands, which would be apt some time or other to cause disorder and ruin.

CHAPTER XIII

Of the Subordination of the Powers of the Commonwealth

§. 149. Though in a constituted commonwealth, standing upon its own basis and acting according to its own nature, that is, acting for the preservation of the community, there can be but *one supreme power,* which is *the legislative,* to which all the rest are and must be subordinate; yet the legislative being only a fiduciary power to act for certain ends, there remains still *in the people a supreme power to remove or alter the legislative* when they find the *legislative* act contrary to the trust reposed in them. For all *power given with trust* for the attaining an *end,* being limited by that end, whenever that *end* is manifestly neglected or opposed, the *trust* must necessarily be *forfeited* and the power devolve into the hands of those that gave it, who may place it anew where they shall think best for their safety and security. And thus the *community* perpetually *retains a supreme power* of saving themselves from the attempts and designs of any body, even of their legislators, whenever they shall be so foolish or so wicked as to lay and carry on designs against the liberties and properties of the subject. For no man or society of men having a power to deliver up their *preservation*, or consequently the means of it, to the absolute will and arbitrary dominion of another, whenever anyone shall go about to bring them into such a slavish condition, they will always have a right to preserve what they have not a power to part with, and to rid themselves of those who invade this fundamental, sacred, and unalterable law of *self-preservation*, for which they entered into society. And thus the *community* may be said in this respect to be *always the supreme power,* but not as considered under any form of government, because this power of the people can never take place until the government be dissolved.

§. 150. In all cases whilst the government subsists, the *legislative is the supreme power.* For what can give laws to another must needs be superior to him. And since the legislative is not otherwise legislative of the society but by the right it has to make laws for all the parts and for every member of the society, prescribing rules to their actions and giving power of execution where they are transgressed, the *legislative* must needs be the *supreme,* and all other powers, in any members or parts of the society, derived from and subordinate to it.

§. 151. In some commonwealths, where the *legislative* is not always in being and the *executive* is vested in a single person who has also a share in the legislative, there that single person in a very tolerable sense may also be called *supreme:* not that he has in himself all the supreme power, which is that of law-making, but because he has in him the *supreme execution* from whom all inferior magistrates derive all their several subordinate powers, or at least the greatest part of them. Having also no legislative superior to him, there being no law to be made without

his consent, which cannot be expected should ever subject him to the other part of the legislative, *he* is properly
enough in this sense *supreme*. But yet it is to be observed
that, though *oaths of allegiance* and fealty are taken to
him, it is not to him as supreme legislator, but as *supreme
executor* of the law, made by a joint power of him with
others. *Allegiance* being nothing but an *obedience according to law,* which when he violates, he has no right to obedience, nor can claim it otherwise than as the public
person vested with the power of the law, and so is to be
considered as the image, phantom, or representative of
the commonwealth, acted by the will of the society,
declared in its laws. And thus he has no will, no power,
but that of the law. But when he quits this representation,
this public will, and acts by his own private will, he
degrades himself and is but a single private person, without power and without will, that has any right to *obedience,* the members owing no *obedience* but to the public
will of the society.

§. 152. The *executive power,* placed anywhere but in a person that has also a share in the legislative, is visibly subordinate and accountable to it and may be at pleasure
changed and displaced; so that it is not the *supreme executive power* that is exempt from *subordination,* but the
supreme executive power vested in one, who having a
share in the legislative, has no distinct superior legislative
to be subordinate and accountable to, farther than he
himself shall join and consent. So that he is no more subordinate than he himself shall think fit, which one may
certainly conclude will be but very little. Of other *ministerial and subordinate powers* in a commonwealth we
need not speak, they being so multiplied with infinite
variety in the different customs and constitutions of distinct commonwealths that it is impossible to give a particular account of them all. Only thus much, which is

necessary to our present purpose, we may take notice of concerning them: that they have no manner of authority, any of them, beyond what is by positive grant and commission delegated to them, and are all of them accountable to some other power in the commonwealth.

§. 153. It is not necessary, no, nor so much as convenient, that the *legislative* should be *always in being,* but absolutely necessary that the executive power should, because there is not always need of new laws to be made, but always need of execution of the laws that are made. When the *legislative* hath put the *execution* of the laws they make into other hands, they have a power still to resume it out of those hands when they find cause and to punish for any mal-administration against the laws. The same holds also in regard of the *federative* power, that and the *executive* being both *ministerial* and *subordinate to the legislative,* which, as has been showed, in a constituted commonwealth is the supreme. The *legislative* also in this case being supposed to consist of several persons (for if it be a single person, it cannot but be always in being, and so will, as supreme, naturally have the supreme executive power, together with the legislative), may *assemble and exercise their legislature* at the times that either their original constitution or their own adjournment appoints, or when they please, if neither of these hath appointed any time or there be no other way prescribed to convoke them. For the supreme power being placed in them by the people, it is always in them and they may exercise it when they please, unless by their original constitution they are limited to certain seasons or by an act of their supreme power they have adjourned to a certain time; and when that time comes, they have a right to *assemble* and act again.

§. 154. If the *legislative,* or any part of it, be made up of *representatives* chosen for that time by the people, which afterwards return into the ordinary state of subject and have no share in the legislature but upon a new choice, this power of choosing must also be exercised by the people, either at certain appointed seasons or else when they are summoned to it. And in this latter case, the power of convoking the legislative is ordinarily placed in the executive and has one of these two limitations in respect of time: that either the original constitution requires their *assembling* and *acting* at certain intervals, and then the executive power does nothing but ministerially issue directions for their electing and assembling according to due forms, or else it is left to his prudence to call them by new elections when the occasions or exigencies of the public require the amendment of old or making of new laws, or the redress or prevention of any inconveniencies that lie on or threaten the people.

§. 155. It may be demanded here, what if the executive power, being possessed of the force of the commonwealth, shall make use of that force to hinder the *meeting* and *acting of the legislative* when the original constitution or the public exigencies require it?° I say, using force upon the people without authority and contrary to the trust put in him that does so, is a state of war with the people, who have a right to *reinstate* their *legislative in the exercise* of their power. For having erected a legislative with an intent they should exercise the power of making laws, either at certain set times or when there is need of it, when they are hindered by any force from what is so necessary to the society, and wherein the safety and preservation of the people consists, the people have a right to remove it by force. In all states and conditions, the true remedy of *force* without authority is to oppose *force* to it. The use of *force* without authority always puts him that uses it into a *state of war,* as the aggressor, and renders him liable to be treated accordingly.

§. 156. The *power of assembling and dismissing the legislative* placed in the executive gives not the executive a superiority over it, but is a fiduciary trust placed in him for the safety of the people, in a case where the uncertainty and variableness of human affairs could not bear a steady fixed rule. For it not being possible that the first framers of the government should, by any foresight, be so much masters of future events as to be able to prefix so just periods of return and duration to the *assemblies of the legislative* in all times to come that might exactly answer all the exigencies of the commonwealth, the best remedy could be found for this defect was to trust this to the prudence of one who was always to be present and whose business it was to watch over the public good. Constant *frequent meetings of the legislative* and long continuations of their assemblies, without necessary occasion, could not but be burdensome to the people and must necessarily in time produce more dangerous inconveniencies, and yet the quick turn of affairs might be sometimes such as to need their present help. Any delay of their *convening* might endanger the public; and sometimes too their business might be so great that the limited time of their sitting might be too short for their work and rob the public of that benefit which could be had only from their mature deliberation. What then could be done in this case to prevent the community from being exposed some time or other to eminent hazard, on one side or the other, by fixed intervals and periods set to the *meeting and acting of the legislative,* but to entrust it to the prudence of some who, being present and acquainted with the state of public affairs, might make use of this prerogative for the public good? And where else could this be so well placed as in his hands who was entrusted with the execution of the laws for the same end? Thus supposing the regulation of times for the *assembling and sitting of the legislative* not settled by the original constitution, it naturally fell into the hands of the executive, not as an arbitrary power depending on his good pleasure, but with this trust: always to have it exercised only for the public weal, as the occurrences of times and change of affairs might require. Whether *settled periods of their convening* or *a liberty* left to the prince for *convoking the legislative,* or perhaps a mixture of both, hath the least inconvenience attending it, it is not my business here to inquire, but only to show that though the executive power may have the prerogative of *convoking* and *dissolving* such *conventions of the legislative,* yet it is not thereby superior to it.

§. 157. Things of this world are in so constant a flux that nothing remains long in the same state. Thus people, riches, trade, power, change their stations, flourishing mighty cities come to ruin and prove in times neglected desolate corners, whilst other unfrequented places grow into populous countries, filled with wealth and inhabitants. But things not always changing equally and private interest often keeping up customs and privileges when the reasons of them are ceased, it often comes to pass that in governments, where part of the legislative consists of *representatives* chosen by the people, that in tract of time this *representation* becomes very *unequal* and disproportionate to the reasons it was at first established upon. To what gross absurdities the following of custom when reason has left it may lead, we may be satisfied, when we see the bare name of a town, of which there remains not so much as the ruins, where scarce so much housing as a sheepcote or more inhabitants than a shepherd is to be found, sends *as many representatives* to the grand assembly of law-makers as a whole county numerous in people and powerful in riches.° This strangers stand amazed at, and everyone must confess needs a remedy; though most think it hard to find one, because the constitution of the legislative being the original and supreme act of the society, antecedent to all positive laws in it and depending wholly on the people, no inferior power can alter it. And therefore the *people,* when the *legislative* is once constituted, *having,* in such a government as we have been speaking of, *no power* to act as long as the government stands, this inconvenience is thought incapable of a remedy.

§. 158. *Salus populi suprema lex,* is certainly so just and fundamental a rule that he who sincerely follows it cannot dangerously err. If therefore the executive, who has the power of convoking the legislative, observing rather the true proportion than fashion of *representation,* regulates, not by old custom but true reason, the *number of members* in all places that have a right to be distinctly represented, which no part of the people however incorporated can pretend to but in proportion to the assistance which it affords to the public, it cannot be judged to have set up a new legislative, but to have restored the old and true one and to have rectified the disorders which succession of time had insensibly, as well as inevitably, introduced. For it being the interest as well as intention of the people to have a fair and *equal representative,* whoever brings it nearest to that is an undoubted friend to and establisher of the government and cannot miss the consent and approbation of the community. *Prerogative* being nothing but a power, in the hands of the prince, to provide for the public good in such cases which, depending upon unforeseen and uncertain occurrences, certain and unalterable laws could not safely direct, whatsoever shall be done manifestly for the good of the people and the establishing the government upon its true foundations is, and always will be, just *prerogative.* The power of

erecting new corporations, and therewith *new represen-*
tatives, carries with it a supposition that in time the *mea-*
sures of representation might vary, and those places have
a just right to be represented which before had none. And
by the same reason those cease to have a right, and be too
inconsiderable for such a privilege, which before had it. It
is not a change from the present state, which perhaps corruption or decay has introduced, that makes an inroad
upon the government, but the tendency of it to injure or
oppress the people and to set up one part or party, with a
distinction from and an unequal subjection of the rest.
Whatsoever cannot but be acknowledged to be of advantage to the society, and people in general, upon just and
lasting measures, will always, when done, justify itself.
And whenever the people shall choose their *representa-*
tives upon just and undeniably *equal measures,* suitable
to the original frame of the government, it cannot be
doubted to be the will and act of the society, whoever
permitted or caused them so to do.

CHAPTER XIV

Of Prerogative

§. 159. Where the legislative and executive power are in distinct hands (as they are in all moderated monarchies and well-framed governments), there the good of the society requires that several things should be left to the discretion of him that has the executive power. For the legislators not being able to foresee and provide by laws for all that may be useful to the community, the executor of the laws, having the power in his hands, has by the common law of nature a right to make use of it for the good of the society in many cases where the municipal law has given no direction, until the legislative can conveniently be assembled to provide for it. Many things there are which the law can by no means provide for; and those must necessarily be left to the discretion of him that has the executive power in his hands, to be ordered by him as the public good and advantage shall require. Nay, it is fit that the laws themselves should in some cases give way to the executive power, or rather to this fundamental law of nature and government, *viz.* that as much as may be *all* the members of the society are to be preserved. For since many accidents may happen, wherein a strict and rigid observation of the laws may do harm (as not to pull down an innocent man's house to stop the fire, when the next to it is burning), and a man may come sometimes within the reach of the law, which makes no distinction of persons, by an action that may deserve reward and pardon, it is fit the ruler should have a power, in many cases, to mitigate the severity of the law and pardon some offenders. For the *end of government* being *the preservation of all,* as much as may be, even the guilty are to be spared where it can prove no prejudice to the innocent.°

§. 160. This power to act according to discretion, for the public good without the prescription of the law, and sometimes even against it, *is* that which is called *prerogative.* For since in some governments the lawmaking power is not always in being and is usually too numerous and so too slow for the dispatch requisite to execution, and because also it is impossible to foresee, and so by laws to provide for, all accidents and necessities that may concern the public or to make such laws as will do no harm if they are executed with an inflexible rigour on all occasions and upon all persons that may come in their way, therefore there is a latitude left to the executive power to do many things of choice which the laws do not prescribe.

§. 161. This power, whilst employed for the benefit of the community and suitably to the trust and ends of the government, *is undoubted prerogative* and never is questioned. For the people are very seldom or never scrupulous or nice in the point. They are far from examining *prerogative* whilst it is in any tolerable degree employed for the use it was meant, that is, for the good of the people, and not manifestly against it. But if there comes to be a *question* between the executive power and the people about a thing claimed as a *prerogative,* the tendency of the exercise of such *prerogative* to the good or hurt of the people will easily decide that question.

§. 162. It is easy to conceive that in the infancy of governments, when commonwealths differed little from families in number of people, they differed from them too but little in number of laws; and the governors, being as the fathers of them, watching over them for their good, the government was almost all *prerogative.* A few established laws served the turn, and the discretion and care of the ruler supplied the rest. But when mistake or flattery prevailed with weak princes to make use of this power for private ends of their own, and not for the public good, the people were fain by express laws to get prerogative determined in those points wherein they found disadvantage from it, and thus declared *limitations of prerogative* were by the people found necessary in cases which they and their ancestors had left, in the utmost latitude, to the wisdom of those princes who made no other but a right use of it, that is, for the good of their people.

§. 163. And therefore they have a very wrong notion of government who say that the people have *encroached upon the prerogative* when they have got any part of it to be defined by positive laws. For in so doing they have not pulled from the prince anything that of right belonged to him, but only declared that that power which they indefinitely left in his or his ancestors hands, to be exercised for their good, was not a thing which they intended him when he used it otherwise. For the end of government being the good of the community, whatsoever alterations are made in it tending to that end cannot be an *encroach-*

ment upon any body, since no body in government can have a right tending to any other end, and those only are *encroachments* which prejudice or hinder the public good. Those who say otherwise speak as if the prince had a distinct and separate interest from the good of the community and was not made for it, the root and source from which spring almost all those evils and disorders which happen in kingly governments. And indeed, if that be so the people under his government are not a society of rational creatures, entered into a community for their mutual good; they are not such as have set rulers over themselves to guard and promote that good, but are to be looked on as an herd of inferior creatures under the dominion of a master, who keeps them and works them for his own pleasure or profit. If men were so void of reason and brutish as to enter into society upon such terms, *prerogative* might indeed be what some men would have it, an arbitrary power to do things hurtful to the people.

§. 164. But since a rational creature cannot be supposed, when free, to put himself into subjection to another for his own harm (though where he finds a good and wise ruler, he may not perhaps think it either necessary or useful to set precise bounds to his power in all things), *prerogative* can be nothing but the people's permitting their rulers to do several things of their own free choice where the law was silent, and sometimes too against the direct letter of the law, for the public good, and their acquiescing in it when so done. For as a good prince, who is mindful of the trust put into his hands and careful of the good of his people, cannot have too much *prerogative,* that is, power to do good, so a weak and ill prince, who would claim that power which his predecessors exercised without the direction of the law as a prerogative belonging to him by right of his office, which he may exercise at his pleasure to make or promote an interest distinct from that of the public, gives the people an occasion to claim their right and limit that power which, whilst it was exercised for their good, they were content should be tacitly allowed.

§. 165. And therefore he that will look into the *history of England* will find that *prerogative* was always *largest* in the hands of our wisest and best princes, because the people, observing the whole tendency of their actions to be the public good, contested not what was done without law to that end. Or if any human frailty or mistake (for princes are but men, made as others) appeared in some small declinations from that end, yet it was visible the main of their conduct tended to nothing but the care of the public. The people, therefore, finding reason to be satisfied with these princes whenever they acted without or contrary to the letter of the law, acquiesced in what they did and, without the least complaint, let them enlarge their *prerogative* as they pleased, judging rightly that they did nothing herein to the prejudice of their laws, since they acted conformable to the foundation and end of all laws, the public good.

§. 166. Such god-like princes indeed had some title to arbitrary power by that argument that would prove absolute monarchy the best government, as that which God himself governs the universe by, because such kings partake of his wisdom and goodness. Upon this is founded that saying, that the reigns of good princes have been always most dangerous to the liberties of their people. For when their successors, managing the government with different thoughts, would draw the actions of those good rulers into precedent and make them the standard of their *prerogative*, as if what had been done only for the good of the people was a right in them to do for the harm of the people if they so pleased, it has often occasioned contest, and sometimes public disorders, before the people could recover their original right and get that to be declared not to be *prerogative* which truly was never so, since it is impossible that anybody in the society should ever have a right to do the people harm; though it be very possible and reasonable that the people should not go about to set any bounds to the *prerogative* of those kings or rulers who themselves transgressed not the bounds of the public good, for *prerogative is nothing but the power of doing public good without a rule.*

§. 167. The power of *calling parliaments* in *England,* as to precise time, place, and duration, is certainly a *prerogative* of the king, but still with this trust, that it shall be made use of for the good of the nation, as the exigencies of the times and variety of occasions shall require. For it being impossible to foresee which should always be the fittest place for them to assemble in and what the best season, the choice of these was left with the executive power, as might be most subservient to the public good and best suit the ends of parliaments.

§. 168. The old question will be asked in this matter of *prerogative,* but *who shall be judge* when this power is made a right use of? I answer: between an executive power in being with such a prerogative, and a legislative that depends upon his will for their convening, there can be no *judge on earth,* as there can be none between the legislative and the people, should either the executive or the legislative, when they have got the power in their hands, design or go about to enslave or destroy them. The people have no other remedy in this, as in all other cases where they have no judge on earth, but to *appeal to heaven.*° For the rulers in such attempts, exercising a power the people never put into their hands (who can never be supposed to consent that anybody should rule over them for their harm), do that which they have not a right to do. And where the body of the people, or any single man, is deprived of their right or is under the exercise of a power without right and have no appeal on earth, then they have a liberty to appeal to heaven whenever they judge the cause of sufficient moment. And therefore, though the *people cannot* be *judge,* so as to have by the constitution of that society any superior power to determine and give effective sentence in the case, yet they have, by a law antecedent and paramount to all positive laws of men, reserved that ultimate determination to themselves which belongs to all mankind where there lies no appeal on earth, *viz.* to judge whether they have just cause to make their appeal to heaven. And this judgment they cannot part with, it being out of a man's power so to submit himself to another as to give him a liberty to destroy him, God and nature never allowing a man so to abandon himself as to neglect his own preservation. And since he cannot take away his own life, neither can he give another power to take it. Nor let anyone think this lays a perpetual foundation for disorder; for this operates not until the inconveniency is so great that the majority feel it, and are weary of it, and find a necessity to have it amended. But this the executive power, or wise princes, never need come in the danger of, and it is the thing of all others they have most need to avoid, as of all others the most perilous.

CHAPTER XV

Of Paternal, Political, and Despotical Power, considered together

§. 169. Though I have had occasion to speak of these separately before, yet the great mistakes of late about government having, as I suppose, arisen from confounding these distinct powers one with another, it may not, perhaps, be amiss to consider them here together.°

§. 170. First, then, *paternal* or *parental power* is nothing but that which parents have over their children, to govern them for the children's good until they come to the use of reason or a state of knowledge wherein they may be supposed capable to understand that rule, whether it be the law of nature or the municipal law of their country, they are to govern themselves by; capable, I say, to know it as well as several others who live as freemen under that law. The affection and tenderness which God hath planted in the breast of parents towards their children makes it evident that this is not intended to be a severe arbitrary government, but only for the help, instruction, and preservation of their offspring. But happen it as it will, there is, as I have proved, no reason why it should be thought to extend to life and death at any time over their children, more than over anybody else. Neither can there be any pretence why this *parental power* should keep the child, when grown to a man, in subjection to the will of his parents any farther than, having received life and education from his parents, obliges him to respect, honour, gratitude, assistance and support, all his life, to both father and mother. And thus it is true the *paternal* is a natural *government*, but not at all extending itself to the ends and jurisdictions of that which is political. The *power of the father doth not reach* at all to the *property* of the child, which is only in his own disposing.

§. 171. *Secondly, political power* is that power which, every man having in the state of nature, has given up into the hands of the society and therein to the governors whom the society hath set over itself, with this express or tacit trust: that it shall be employed for their good and the preservation of their property. Now this *power,* which every man has *in the state of nature* and which he parts with to the society in all such cases where the society can secure him, is to use such means for the preserving of his own property as he thinks good and nature allows him, and to punish the breach of the law of nature in others, so as (according to the best of his reason) may most conduce to the preservation of himself and the rest of mankind. So that the *end and measure of this power,* when in every man's hands in the state of nature, being the preservation of all of his society, that is, all mankind in general, it can have no other *end or measure,* when in the hands of the magistrate, but to preserve the members of that society in their lives, liberties, and possessions; and so cannot be an absolute, arbitrary power over their lives and fortunes, which are as much as possible to be preserved, but a *power to make laws* and annex such *penalties* to them as may tend to the preservation of the whole, by cutting off those parts, and those only, which are so corrupt that they threaten the sound and healthy, without which no severity is lawful. And this *power has its original only from compact* and agreement and the mutual consent of those who make up the community.

§. 172. *Thirdly, despotical power* is an absolute, arbitrary power one man has over another to take away his life whenever he pleases. This is a power which neither nature gives, for it has made no such distinction between one man and another, nor compact can convey. For man not having such an arbitrary power over his own life, cannot give another man such a power over it; but it is the *effect only of forfeiture,* which the aggressor makes of his own life when he puts himself into the state of war with another. For having quitted reason, which God hath given to be the rule between man and man and the common bond whereby human kind is united into one fellowship and society, and having renounced the way of peace which that teaches and made use of the force of war to compass his unjust ends upon another where he has no right, and so revolting from his own kind to that of beasts, by making force, which is theirs, to be his rule of right, he renders himself liable to be destroyed by the injured person and the rest of mankind that will join with him in the execution of justice, as any other wild beast or noxious brute with whom mankind can have neither society nor security.[1] And thus *captives* taken in a just and lawful war, and such only, are *subject to a despotical power,* which, as it arises not from compact, so neither is it capable of any, but is the state of war contin-

---

1. Another copy corrected by Mr. Locke, has it thus, *Noxious brute that is destructive to their being.* (Editor's note to the 1764 edition)

ued. For what compact can be made with a man that is not master of his own life, what condition can he perform? And if he be once allowed to be master of his own life, the *despotical, arbitrary power* of his master ceases. He that is master of himself and his own life has a right too to the means of preserving it; so that *as soon as compact enters, slavery ceases,* and he so far quits his absolute power and puts an end to the state of war who enters into conditions with his captive.

§. 173. *Nature gives* the first of these, *viz. paternal power to parents* for the benefit of their children during their minority, to supply their want of ability and understanding how to manage their property. (By *property* I must be understood here, as in other places, to mean that property which men have in their persons as well as goods.) *Voluntary agreement gives* the second, *viz. political power to governors* for the benefit of their subjects, to secure them in the possession and use of their properties. And *forfeiture gives* the third, *despotical power to lords* for their own benefit over those who are stripped of all property.

§. 174. He that shall consider the distinct rise and extent and the different ends of these several powers will plainly see that *paternal power* comes as far short of that of the *magistrate* as *despotical* exceeds it, and that *absolute dominion,* however placed, is so far from being one kind of civil society that it is as inconsistent with it, as slavery is with property. *Paternal power* is only where minority makes the child incapable to manage his property; *political,* where men have property in their own disposal; and *despotical,* over such as have no property at all.

CHAPTER XVI

Of Conquest

§. 175. Though governments can originally have no other rise than that before mentioned nor *polities* be *founded on* anything but *the consent of the people,* yet such have been the disorders ambition has filled the world with, that in the noise of war, which makes so great a part of the history of mankind, *this consent* is little taken notice of. And therefore many have mistaken the force of arms for the consent of the people and reckon conquest as one of the originals of government.° But *conquest* is as far from setting up any government as demolishing a house is from building a new one in the place. Indeed, it often makes way for a new frame of a commonwealth by destroying the former, but, without the consent of the people, can never erect a new one.

§. 176. That the *aggressor* who puts himself into the state of war with another and *unjustly invades* another man's right, *can,* by such an unjust war, *never* come to *have a right over the conquered* will be easily agreed by all men who will not think that robbers and pirates have a right of empire over whomsoever they have force enough to master, or that men are bound by promises which unlawful force extorts from them. Should a robber break into my house, and with a dagger at my throat make me seal deeds to convey my estate to him, would this give him any title? Just such a title, by his sword, has an *unjust conqueror* who forces me into submission. The injury and the crime is equal, whether committed by the wearer of a crown or some petty villain. The title of the offender and the number of his followers make no difference in the offence, unless it be to aggravate it. The only difference is great robbers punish little ones, to keep them in their obedience; but the great ones are rewarded with laurels and triumphs, because they are too big for the weak hands of justice in this world and have the power in their own possession which should punish offenders. What is my remedy against a robber that so broke into my house? *Appeal* to the law for justice. But perhaps justice is denied or I am crippled and cannot stir, robbed and have not the means to do it. If God has taken away all means of seeking remedy, there is nothing left but patience. But my son, when able, may seek the relief of the law which I am denied. He or his son may renew his *appeal* until he recover his right. But the conquered or their children have no court, no arbitrator on earth to appeal to. Then they may *appeal*, as *Jephtha* did, *to heaven* and repeat their *appeal* until they have recovered the native right of their ancestors, which was to have such a legislative over them as the majority should approve and freely acquiesce in. If it be objected, this would cause endless trouble, I answer, no more than justice does where she lies open to all that appeal to her. He that troubles his neighbour without a cause is punished for it by the justice of the court he appeals to. And he that *appeals to heaven* must be sure he has right on his side, and a right too that is worth the trouble and cost of the appeal, as he will answer at a tribunal that cannot be deceived and will be sure to retribute to everyone according to the mischiefs he hath created to his fellow subjects, that is, any part of mankind. From whence it is plain that he that *conquers in an unjust war can thereby have no title to the subjection and obedience of the conquered.*

§. 177. But supposing victory favours the right side, let us consider a *conqueror in a lawful war* and see what power he gets and over whom.

First, it is plain he *gets no power by his conquest over those that conquered with him.* They that fought on his side cannot suffer by the conquest, but must at least be as much freemen as they were before. And most commonly they serve upon terms and on condition to share with their leader and enjoy a part of the spoil and other advantages that attend the conquering sword, or at least have a part of the subdued country bestowed upon them. And *the conquering people are not, I hope, to be slaves by conquest* and wear their laurels only to show they are sacrifices to their leader's triumph. They that found absolute monarchy upon the title of the sword make their heroes, who are the founders of such monarchies, arrant *Drawcan-sirs* and forget they had any officers and soldiers that fought on their side in the battles they won, or assisted them in the subduing, or shared in possessing the countries they mastered. We are told by some that the *English* monarchy is founded in the *Norman* conquest and that our princes have thereby a title to absolute dominion: which if it were true (as by the history it appears otherwise), and that *William* had a right to make war on this island, yet his dominion by conquest could reach no farther than to the *Saxons* and *Britons* that were then inhabitants of this country. The *Normans* that came with him and helped to conquer, and all descended from them, are freemen and no subjects by conquest, let that give what dominion it will. And if I or anybody else shall claim freedom, as derived from them, it will be very hard to prove the contrary. And it is plain the law, that has made no distinction between the one and the other, intends not there should be any difference in their freedom or privileges.

§. 178. But supposing, which seldom happens, that the conquerors and conquered never incorporate into one people, under the same laws and freedom: let us see next *what power a lawful conqueror has over the subdued*. And that I say is purely despotical. He has an absolute power over the lives of those who by an unjust war have forfeited them, but not over the lives or fortunes of those who engaged not in the war, nor over the possessions even of those who were actually engaged in it.

§. 179. *Secondly*, I say then the *conqueror* gets no power but only over those who have actually assisted, concurred, or consented to that unjust force that is used against him. For the people having given to their governors no power to do an unjust thing, such as is to make an unjust war (for they never had such a power in themselves), they ought not to be charged as guilty of the violence and injustice that is committed in an unjust war, any farther than they actually abet it, no more than they are to be thought guilty of any violence or oppression their governors should use upon the people themselves, or any part of their fellow subjects, they having empowered them no more to the one than to the other. Conquerors, it is true, seldom trouble themselves to make the distinction, but they willingly permit the confusion of war to sweep all together; but yet this alters not the right. For the conqueror's power over the lives of the conquered, being only because they have used force to do or maintain an injustice, he can have that power only over those who have concurred in that force. All the rest are innocent. And he has no more title over the people of that country who have done him no injury, and so have made no forfeiture of their lives, than he has over any other who, without any injuries or provocations, have lived upon fair terms with him.°

§. 180. *Thirdly,* the *power a conqueror gets* over those he overcomes *in a just war is perfectly despotical:* he has an absolute power over the lives of those, who, by putting themselves in a state of war, have forfeited them. But he has not thereby a right and title to their possessions. This I doubt not but at first sight will seem a strange doctrine, it being so quite contrary to the practice of the world; there being nothing more familiar in speaking of the dominion of countries than to say, such an one conquered it. As if conquest, without any more ado, conveyed a right of possession. But when we consider that the practice of the strong and powerful, how universal soever it may be, is seldom the rule of right, however it be one part of the subjection of the conquered not to argue against the conditions cut out to them by the conquering sword.

§. 181. Though in all war there be usually a complication of force and damage, and the aggressor seldom fails to harm the estate when he uses force against the persons of those he makes war upon; yet it is the use of force only that puts a man into the state of war. For whether by force he begins the injury, or else having quietly and by fraud done the injury, he refuses to make reparation and by force maintains it (which is the same thing as at first to have done it by force), it is the unjust use of force that makes the war. For he that breaks open my house and violently turns me out of doors or, having peaceably got in, by force keeps me out, does in effect the same thing, supposing we are in such a state that we have no common judge on earth whom I may appeal to and to whom we are both obliged to submit. For of such I am now speaking. It is the *unjust use of force*, then, that *puts a man into the state of war* with another; and thereby he that is guilty of it makes a forfeiture of his life. For quitting reason, which is the rule given between man and man, and using force, the way of beasts, he becomes liable to be destroyed by him he uses force against, as any savage ravenous beast that is dangerous to his being.

§. 182. But because the miscarriages of the father are no faults of the children, and they may be rational and peaceable notwithstanding the brutishness and injustice of the father, the father, by his miscarriages and violence, can forfeit but his own life, but involves not his children in his guilt or destruction. His goods, which nature, that willeth the preservation of all mankind as much as is possible, hath made to belong to the children to keep them from perishing, do still continue to belong to his children. For supposing them not to have joined in the war, either through infancy, absence, or choice, they have done nothing to forfeit them. N*or has the conqueror any right* to take them away by the bare title of having subdued him that by force attempted his destruction, though perhaps he may have some right to them to repair the damages he has sustained by the war and the defence of his own right, which how far it reaches to the possessions of the conquered, we shall see by and by. So that he that *by conquest has a right over a man's person* to destroy him if he pleases, has *not* thereby a right over *his estate* to possess and enjoy it. For it is the brutal force the aggressor has used that gives his adversary a right to take away his life and destroy him if he pleases, as a noxious creature;

but it is damage sustained that alone gives him title to another man's goods. For though I may kill a thief that sets on me in the highway, yet I may not (which seems less) take away his money and let him go. This would be robbery on my side. His force and the state of war he put himself in made him forfeit his life, but gave me no title to his goods.° The *right* then of *conquest extends only to the lives* of those who joined in the war, *not to their estates,* but only in order to make reparation for the damages received and the charges of the war, and that too with reservation of the right of the innocent wife and children.

§. 183. Let the *conqueror* have as much justice on his side as could be supposed, he *has no right* to seize more than the vanquished could forfeit: his life is at the victor's mercy, and his service and goods he may appropriate to make himself reparation. But he cannot take the goods of his wife and children. They too had a title to the goods he enjoyed and their shares in the estate he possessed. For example, I in the state of nature (and all commonwealths are in the state of nature one with another) have injured another man, and refusing to give satisfaction, it comes to a state of war wherein my defending by force what I had gotten unjustly makes me the aggressor. I am conquered. My life, it is true, as forfeit is at mercy, but not my wife's and children's. They made not the war nor assisted in it. I could not forfeit their lives; they were not mine to forfeit. My wife had a share in my estate; that neither could I forfeit. And my children also, being born of me, had a right to be maintained out of my labour or substance. Here then is the case: the conqueror has a title to reparation for damages received, and the children have a title to their father's estate for their subsistence. For as to the wife's share, whether her own labour or compact gave her a title to it, it is plain her husband could not forfeit what was hers. What must be done in the case? I answer: the fundamental law of nature being that all, as much as may be, should be preserved, it follows that if there be not enough fully to *satisfy* both, *viz.* for the *conqueror's losses* and children's maintenance, he that hath and to spare must remit something of his full satisfaction and give way to the pressing and preferable title of those who are in danger to perish without it.°

§. 184. But supposing the *charge* and *damages of the war* are to be made up to the conqueror to the utmost farthing, and that the children of the vanquished, spoiled of all their father's goods, are to be left to starve and perish; yet the satisfying of what shall, on this score, be due to the conqueror will scarce give him a *title to any country he shall conquer.* For the damages of war can scarce amount to the value of any considerable tract of land, in any part of the world where all the land is possessed and none lies waste. And if I have not taken away the conqueror's land, which, being vanquished, it is impossible I should, scarce any other spoil I have done him can amount to the value of mine, supposing it equally cultivated and of an extent any way coming near what I had overrun of his. The destruction of a year's product or two (for it seldom reaches four or five) is the utmost spoil that usually can be done. For as to money and such riches and treasure taken away, these are none of nature's goods. They have but a fantastical imaginary value. Nature has put no such upon them; they are of no more account by her standard than the wampompeke of the *Americans* to an *European* prince or the silver money of *Europe* would have been formerly to an *American*. And five years' product is not worth the perpetual inheritance of land, where all is possessed and none remains waste, to be taken up by him that is disseized; which will be easily granted if one do but take away the imaginary value of money, the disproportion being more than between five and five hundred. Though, at the same time, half a year's product is more worth than the inheritance, where there being more land than the inhabitants possess and make use of, anyone has liberty to make use of the waste. But there conquerors take little care to possess themselves of the *lands of the vanquished*. No damage, therefore, that men in the state of nature (as all princes and governments are in reference to one another) suffer from one another can give a conqueror power to dispossess the posterity of the vanquished and turn them out of that inheritance which ought to be the possession of them and their descendants to all generations. The conqueror indeed will be apt to think himself master, and it is the very condition of the subdued not to be able to dispute their right. But if that be all, it gives no other title than what bare force gives to the stronger over the weaker. And by this reason, he that is strongest will have a right to whatever he pleases to seize on.

§. 185. Over those then that joined with him in the war and over those of the subdued country that opposed him not, and the posterity even of those that did, the conqueror, even in a just war, hath, by his conquest, no *right of dominion*. They are free from any subjection to him, and if their former government be dissolved, they are at liberty to begin and erect another to themselves.

§. 186. The conqueror, it is true, usually by the force he has over them, compels them with a sword at their breasts to stoop to his conditions and submit to such a government as he pleases to afford them; but the enquiry is, what right he has to do so? If it be said, they submit by their own consent, then this allows their own *consent* to be *necessary to give the conqueror a title to rule* over them. It remains only to be considered whether *promises extorted by force,* without right, can be thought consent and *how far they bind*. To which I shall say, they *bind not at all;* because whatsoever another gets from me by force I still retain the right of, and he is obliged presently to restore. He that forces my horse from me ought presently to restore him, and I have still a right to retake him. By the same reason, he that *forced a promise* from me ought presently to restore it, *i. e.* quit me of the obligation of it; or I may resume it myself, *i. e.* choose whether I will perform it. For the law of nature, laying an obligation on me only by the rules she prescribes, cannot oblige me by the violation of her rules: such is the extorting anything from me by force. Nor does it at all alter the case to say, *I gave my promise,* no more than it excuses the force and passes the right when I put my hand in my pocket and deliver my purse myself to a thief, who demands it with a pistol at my breast.

§. 187. From all which it follows that the *government of a conqueror,* imposed by force on the subdued against whom he had no right of war or who joined not in the war against him where he had right, *has no obligation* upon them.

§. 188. But let us suppose that all the men of that community, being all members of the same body politic, may be taken to have joined in that unjust war wherein they are subdued, and so their lives are at the mercy of the conqueror.

§. 189. I say, this concerns not their children who are in their minority. For since a father hath not in himself a power over the life or liberty of his child, no act of his can possibly forfeit it. So that the children, whatever may have happened to the fathers, are freemen, and the absolute power of the *conqueror* reaches no farther than the persons of the men that were subdued by him and dies with them. And should he govern them as slaves, subjected to his absolute arbitrary power, he *has no such right of dominion over their children.* He can have no power over them but by their own consent, whatever he may drive them to say or do, and he has no lawful authority whilst force, and not choice, compels them to submission.

§. 190. Every man is born with a double right: *first,* a *right of freedom to his person,* which no other man has a power over, but the free disposal of it lies in himself. *Secondly,* a *right,* before any other man, *to inherit* with his brethren his *father's goods.*°

§. 191. By the first of these, a man is *naturally free* from subjection to any government, though he be born in a place under its jurisdiction. But if he disclaim the lawful government of the country he was born in, he must also quit the right that belonged to him by the laws of it and the possessions there descending to him from his ancestors, if it were a government made by their consent.

§. 192. By the second, the *inhabitants* of any country who are descended and derive a title to their estates from those who are subdued and had a government forced upon them against their free consents, *retain a right to the possession of their ancestors,* though they consent not freely to the government, whose hard conditions were by force imposed on the possessors of that country. For the first *conqueror never having had a title to the land* of that country, the people who are the descendants of, or claim under those, who were forced to submit to the yoke of a government by constraint, have always a right to shake it off and free themselves from the usurpation or tyranny which the sword hath brought in upon them, until their rulers put them under such a frame of government as they willingly and of choice consent to. Who doubts but the Grecian Christians, descendants of the ancient possessors of that country, may justly cast off the Turkish yoke which they have so long groaned under, whenever they have an opportunity to do it? For no government can have a right to obedience from a people who have not freely consented to it, which they can never be supposed to do until either they are put in a full state of liberty to choose their government and governors, or at least until they have such standing laws to which they have by themselves or their representatives given their free consent; and also until they are allowed their due property, which is so to be proprietors of what they have that nobody can take away any part of it without their own consent, without which men under any government are not in the state of freemen, but are direct slaves under the force of war.

§. 193. But granting that the *conqueror* in a just war has a right to the estates, as well as power over the persons, of the conquered, which it is plain he *hath* not: nothing of *absolute power* will follow from hence in the continuance of the government. Because the descendants of these being all freemen, if he grants them estates and possessions to inhabit his country (without which it would be worth nothing), whatsoever he grants them they have, so far as it is granted, *property* in. The nature whereof is that *without a man's own consent* it *cannot be taken from him.*

§. 194. Their *persons* are *free* by a native right, and their *properties,* be they more or less, are *their own and at their own dispose* and not at his, or else it is no *property.* Supposing the conqueror gives to one man a thousand acres, to him and his heirs forever, to another he lets a thousand acres for his life, under the rent of 50 l. or 500 l. *per ann.,* has not the one of these a right to his thousand acres for ever, and the other, during his life, paying the said rent? And hath not the tenant for life a *property* in all that he gets over and above his rent by his labour and industry during the said term, supposing it be double the rent? Can anyone say the king or conqueror, after his grant, may by his power of conqueror take away all or part of the land from the heirs of one, or from the other during his life, he paying the rent? Or can he take away from either the goods or money they have got upon the said land, at his pleasure? If he can, then all free and voluntary *contracts* cease and are void in the world. There needs nothing to dissolve them at any time but power enough, and all the *grants* and *promises* of *men in power* are but mockery and collusion. For can there be anything more ridiculous than to say, I give you and yours this forever, and that in the surest and most solemn way of conveyance can be devised, and yet it is to be understood that I have right, if I please, to take it away from you again tomorrow?

§. 195. I will not dispute now whether princes are exempt from the laws of their country. But this I am sure, they owe subjection to the laws of God and nature. No body, no power, can exempt them from the obligations of that eternal law. Those are so great and so strong in the case of *promises*, that omnipotency itself can be tied by them. *Grants, promises,* and *oaths* are *bonds* that *hold the Almighty,* whatever some flatterers say to princes of the world, who all together, with all their people joined to them, are, in comparison of the great God, but as a drop of the bucket or a dust on the balance, inconsiderable, nothing!

§. 196. The short of the *case in conquest* is this: the conqueror, if he have a just cause, has a despotical right over the persons of all that actually aided and concurred in the war against him, and a right to make up his damage and cost out of their labour and estates, so he injure not the right of any other. Over the rest of the people, if there were any that consented not to the war, and over the children of the captives themselves or the possessions of either, he has no power; and so can have, *by virtue of conquest, no lawful title* himself *to dominion* over them or derive it to his posterity, but is an aggressor if he attempts upon their properties, and thereby puts himself in a state of war against them and has no better a right of principality, he, nor any of his successors, than *Hingar,* or *Hubba,* the Danes, had here in *England,* or *Spartacus,* had he conquered *Italy,* would have had: which is to have their yoke cast off, as soon as God shall give those under their subjection courage and opportunity to do it. Thus, notwithstanding whatever title the kings of *Assyria* had over *Judah* by the sword, God assisted *Hezekiah* to throw off the dominion of that conquering empire. *And the lord was with Hezekiah, and he prospered; wherefore he went forth, and he rebelled against the king of Assyria, and served him not,* 2 Kings xviii. 7. Whence it is plain that shaking off a power which force, and not right, hath set over any one, though it hath the name of *rebellion,* yet is no offence before God, but is that which he allows and countenances, though even promises and covenants, when obtained by force, have intervened. For it is very probable, to any one that reads the story of *Ahaz* and *Hezekiah* attentively, that the *Assyrians* subdued *Ahaz* and deposed him and made *Hezekiah* king in his father's lifetime, and that *Hezekiah* by agreement had done him homage and paid him tribute all this time.

CHAPTER XVII

Of Usurpation

§. 197. As conquest may be called a foreign usurpation, so usurpation is a kind of domestic conquest, with this difference: that an usurper can never have right on his side, it being no *usurpation* but where one is got into the *possession of what another has right to*. This, so far as it is *usurpation*, is a change only of persons, but not of the forms and rules of the government. For if the usurper extend his power beyond what of right belonged to the lawful princes or governors of the commonwealth, it is *tyranny* added to *usurpation*.

§. 198. In all lawful governments the designation of the persons who are to bear rule is as natural and necessary a part as the form of the government itself, and is that which had its establishment originally from the people. Hence all commonwealths with the form of government established have rules also of appointing those who are to have any share in the public authority and settled methods of conveying the right to them. For the anarchy is much alike to have no form of government at all, or to agree that it shall be monarchical, but to appoint no way to know or design the person that shall have the power and be the monarch. Whoever gets into the exercise of any part of the power by other ways than what the laws of the community have prescribed hath no right to be obeyed, though the form of the commonwealth be still preserved, since he is not the person the laws have appointed and consequently not the person the people have consented to. Nor can such an *usurper,* or any deriving from him, ever have a title until the people are both at liberty to consent and have actually consented to allow and confirm in him the power he hath until then usurped.

CHAPTER XVIII

Of Tyranny

§. 199. As usurpation is the exercise of power which another hath a right to, so *tyranny is the exercise of power beyond right,* which nobody can have a right to.° And this is making use of the power anyone has in his hands, not for the good of those who are under it, but for his own private separate advantage, when the governor, however titled, makes not the law but his will the rule, and his commands and actions are not directed to the preservation of the properties of his people, but the satisfaction of his own ambition, revenge, covetousness, or any other irregular passion.

§. 200. If one can doubt this to be truth or reason because it comes from the obscure hand of a subject, I hope the authority of a king will make it pass with him. King *James* the first, in his speech to the parliament, 1603, tells them thus, *I will ever prefer the weal of the public, and of the whole commonwealth, in making of good laws and*

*constitutions, to any particular and private ends of mine;
thinking ever the wealth and weal of the commonwealth to
be my greatest weal and worldly felicity; a point wherein a
lawful king doth directly differ from a tyrant.* For I do
acknowledge, that the special and greatest point of difference that is between a rightful king and an usurping
tyrant, is this, that whereas the proud and ambitious
tyrant doth think his kingdom and people are only
ordained for satisfaction of his desires and unreasonable
appetites, the righteous and just king doth by the contrary
acknowledge himself to be ordained for the procuring of
the wealth and property of his people. And again, in his
speech to the parliament, 1609, he hath these words, *The
king binds himself by a double oath, to the observation of
the fundamental laws of his kingdom; tacitly, as by being a
king, and so bound to protect as well the people, as the
laws of his kingdom; and expressly, by his oath at his coro-
nation; so as every just king, in a settled kingdom, is bound
to observe that paction made to his people, by his laws, in
framing his government agreeable thereunto, according to
that paction which God made with* Noah *after the deluge.
Hereafter, seed-time and harvest, and cold and heat, and
summer and winter, and day and night, shall not cease
while the earth remaineth. And therefore a king governing
in a settled kingdom, leaves to be a king, and degenerates
into a tyrant, as soon as he leaves off to rule according to
his laws.* And a little after, *Therefore all kings that are not
tyrants, or perjured, will be glad to bound themselves
within the limits of their laws; and they that persuade
them the contrary, are vipers, and pests both against them
and the commonwealth.* Thus that learned king, who well
understood the notion of things, makes the difference
between a *king* and a *tyrant* to consist only in this, that
one makes the laws the bounds of his power and the good
of the public the end of his government; the other makes
all give way to his own will and appetite.

§. 201. It is a mistake to think this fault is proper only to monarchies; other forms of government are liable to it, as well as that. For wherever the power, that is put in any hands for the government of the people and the preservation of their properties, is applied to other ends and made use of to impoverish, harass, or subdue them to the arbitrary and irregular commands of those that have it, there it presently becomes *tyranny*, whether those that thus use it are one or many. Thus we read of the thirty tyrants at *Athens*, as well as one at *Syracuse;* and the intolerable dominion of the *Decemviri* at *Rome* was nothing better.

§. 202. *Wherever law ends, tyranny begins,* if the law be transgressed to another's harm. And whosoever in authority exceeds the power given him by the law and makes use of the force he has under his command to compass that upon the subject which the law allows not, ceases in that to be a magistrate, and, acting without authority, may be opposed, as any other man who by force invades the right of another. This is acknowledged in subordinate magistrates. He that hath authority to seize my person in the street may be opposed as a thief and a robber if he endeavours to break into my house to execute a writ, notwithstanding that I know he has such a warrant and such a legal authority as will empower him to arrest me abroad. And why this should not hold in the highest, as well as in the most inferior magistrate, I would gladly be informed. Is it reasonable that the eldest brother, because he has the greatest part of his father's estate, should thereby have a right to take away any of his younger brothers' portions, or that a rich man, who possessed a whole country, should from thence have a right to seize, when he pleased, the cottage and garden of his poor neighbour? The being rightfully possessed of great power and riches, exceedingly beyond the greatest part of the sons of *Adam*, is so far from being an excuse, much less a reason, for rapine and oppression, which damaging another without authority is, that it is a great aggravation of it. For the exceeding the bounds of authority is no more a right in a great than in a petty officer, no more justifiable in a king than a constable, but is so much the worse in him, in that he has more trust put in him, has already a much greater share than the rest of his brethren, and is supposed, from the advantages of his education, employment, and counsellors, to be more knowing in the measures of right and wrong.

§. 203. May the *commands* then *of a prince be opposed?* May he be resisted as often as anyone shall find himself aggrieved and but imagine he has not right done him? This will unhinge and overturn all polities, and instead of government and order, leave nothing but anarchy and confusion.

§. 204. To this I answer, that *force* is to be *opposed* to nothing but to unjust and unlawful *force;* whoever makes any opposition in any other case draws on himself a just condemnation both from God and man. And so no such danger or confusion will follow, as is often suggested, for:

§. 205. *First,* as in some countries, the person of the prince by the law is sacred, and so whatever he commands or does, his person is still free from all question or violence, not liable to force or any judicial censure or condemnation. But yet opposition may be made to the illegal acts of any inferior officer or other commissioned by him, unless he will, by actually putting himself into a state of war with his people, dissolve the government and leave them to that defence which belongs to everyone in the state of nature. For of such things who can tell what the end will be? And a neighbour kingdom has showed the world an odd example. In all other cases the *sacred-*

ness of the *person exempts him from all inconveniencies,*
whereby he is secure, whilst the government stands, from
all violence and harm whatsoever, than which there cannot be a wiser constitution. For the harm he can do in his
own person not being likely to happen often nor to extend
itself far, nor being able by his single strength to subvert
the laws nor oppress the body of the people, should any
prince have so much weakness and ill nature as to be
willing to do it, the inconveniency of some particular
mischiefs that may happen sometimes, when a heady
prince comes to the throne, are well recompensed by the
peace of the public, and security of the government, in
the person of the chief magistrate, thus set out of the
reach of danger: it being safer for the body that some few
private men should be sometimes in danger to suffer
than that the head of the republic should be easily and
upon slight occasions exposed.

§. 206. *Secondly,* but this privilege, belonging only to the
king's person, hinders not but they may be questioned,
opposed, and resisted who use unjust force, though they
pretend a commission from him which the law authorizes not; as is plain in the case of him that has the king's
writ to arrest a man, which is a full commission from the
king. And yet he that has it cannot break open a man's
house to do it, nor execute this command of the king
upon certain days, nor in certain places, though this
commission have no such exception in it; but they are the
limitations of the law, which if any one transgress, the
king's commission excuses him not. For the king's
authority being given him only by the law, he cannot
empower anyone to act against the law, or justify him, by
his commission, in so doing, the *commission* or *command of any magistrate, where he has no authority,* being
as *void* and insignificant as that of any private man. The
difference between the one and the other being that the

magistrate has some authority so far, and to such ends, and the private man has none at all. For it is not the *commission*, but the *authority*, that gives the right of acting, and *against the laws there can be no authority*. But, notwithstanding such resistance, the king's person and authority are still both secured and so *no danger to governor or government*.

§. 207. *Thirdly*, supposing a government wherein the person of the chief magistrate is not thus sacred: yet this *doctrine* of the lawfulness of *resisting* all unlawful exercises of his power *will not* upon every slight occasion endanger him or *embroil the government*. For where the injured party may be relieved and his damages repaired by appeal to the law, there can be no pretence for force, which is only to be used where a man is intercepted from appealing to the law. For nothing is to be accounted hostile force but where it leaves not the remedy of such an appeal. And it is such *force* alone that *puts* him that uses it *into a state of war* and makes it lawful to resist him. A man with a sword in his hand demands my purse in the highway when perhaps I have not twelve pence in my pocket. This man I may lawfully kill. To another I deliver 100 l. to hold only whilst I alight, which he refuses to restore me when I am got up again, but draws his sword to defend the possession of it by force if I endeavour to retake it. The mischief this man does me is a hundred, or possibly a thousand, times more than the other perhaps intended me (whom I killed before he really did me any); and yet I might lawfully kill the one and cannot so much as hurt the other lawfully. The reason whereof is plain: because the one, using *force* which threatened my life, I could not have *time to appeal* to the law to secure it; and when it was gone, it was too late to appeal. The law could not restore life to my dead carcass; the loss was irreparable, which to prevent the law of nature gave me a right to *destroy* him, who had put himself into a state of war with me, and threatened my destruction. But in the other case, my life not being in danger, I may have the *benefit of appealing* to the law and have reparation for my 100 l. that way.

§. 208. *Fourthly,* but if the unlawful acts done by the magistrate be maintained (by the power he has got), and the remedy which is due by law be by the same power obstructed, yet the *right of resisting,* even in such manifest acts of tyranny, *will not* suddenly or on slight occasions *disturb the government.* For if it reach no farther than some private men's cases, though they have a right to defend themselves and to recover by force what by unlawful force is taken from them, yet the right to do so will not easily engage them in a contest wherein they are sure to perish, it being as impossible for one or a few oppressed men to *disturb the government,* where the body of the people do not think themselves concerned in it, as for a raving madman or heady malcontent to overturn a well-settled state, the people being as little apt to follow the one as the other.

§. 209. But if either these illegal acts have extended to the majority of the people, or if the mischief and oppression has lighted only on some few, but in such cases as the precedent and consequences seem to threaten all, and they are persuaded in their consciences that their laws, and with them their estates, liberties, and lives are in danger, and perhaps their religion too, how they will be hindered from resisting illegal force used against them I cannot tell. This is an *inconvenience,* I confess, *that attends all governments* whatsoever, when the governors have brought it to this pass to be generally suspected of their people, the most dangerous state which they can possibly put themselves in; wherein they are the less to be pitied because it is so easy to be avoided, it being as impossible for a governor, if he really means the good of his people and the preservation of them and their laws together, not to make them see and feel it, as it is for the father of a family not to let his children see he loves and takes care of them.

§. 210. But if all the world shall observe pretences of one kind and actions of another, arts used to elude the law and the trust of prerogative (which is an arbitrary power in some things left in the prince's hand to do good, not harm to the people) employed contrary to the end for which it was given; if the people shall find the ministers and subordinate magistrates chosen suitable to such ends and favoured or laid by, proportionably as they promote or oppose them; if they see several experiments made of arbitrary power, and that religion underhand favoured (though publicly proclaimed against) which is readiest to introduce it,° and the operators in it supported, as much as may be, and when that cannot be done, yet approved still and liked the better: if a *long train of actions show the councils* all tending that way, how can a man any more hinder himself from being persuaded in his own mind which way things are going, or from casting about how to save himself, than he could from believing the captain of the ship he was in was carrying him and the rest of the company to *Algiers,* when he found him always steering that course, though cross winds, leaks in his ship, and want of men and provisions did often force him to turn his course another way for some time, which he steadily returned to again, as soon as the wind, weather, and other circumstances would let him?

CHAPTER XIX

Of the Dissolution of Government

§. 211. He that will with any clearness speak of the *dissolution of government* ought in the first place to distinguish between the *dissolution of the society* and the *dissolution of the government.* That which makes the community and brings men out of the loose state of nature into *one politic society* is the agreement which everyone has with the rest to incorporate and act as one body, and so be one distinct commonwealth.° The usual and almost only way whereby *this union is dissolved* is the inroad of foreign force making a conquest upon them. For in that case (not being able to maintain and support themselves as *one entire* and *independent body*) the union belonging to that body which consisted therein must necessarily cease, and so everyone return to the state he was in before with a liberty to shift for himself and provide for his own safety, as he thinks fit, in some other society. Whenever the *society is dissolved,* it is certain the government of that society cannot remain. Thus conquerors' swords often cut up governments by the roots and mangle societies to pieces, separating the subdued or scattered multitude from the protection of and dependence on that society which ought to have preserved them from violence. The world is too well instructed in, and too forward to allow of, this way of dissolving of governments to need any more to be said of it. And there wants not much argument to prove that where the *society is dissolved,* the government cannot remain, that being as impossible as for the frame of an house to subsist when the materials of it are scattered and dissipated by a whirlwind or jumbled into a confused heap by an earthquake.

§. 212. Besides this overturning from without, *governments are dissolved from within:*

First, when the *legislative* is *altered.* Civil society being a state of peace amongst those who are of it, from whom the state of war is excluded by the umpirage which they have provided in their legislative for the ending all differences that may arise amongst any of them, it is in their *legislative* that the members of a commonwealth are united and combined together into one coherent living body. This *is the soul that gives form, life, and unity* to the commonwealth. From hence the several members have their mutual influence, sympathy, and connexion. And, therefore, when the *legislative* is broken or *dissolved,* dissolution and death follows. For the *essence and union of the society* consisting in having one will, the legislative, when once established by the majority, has the declaring and as it were keeping of that will. The *constitution of the legislative* is the first and fundamental act of society, whereby provision is made for the *continuation of their union* under the direction of persons and bonds of laws made by persons authorized thereunto by the consent and appointment of the people, without which no one man, or number of men, amongst them can have authority of making laws that shall be binding to the rest. When any one or more shall take upon them to make laws whom the people have not appointed so to do, they make laws without authority which the people are not therefore bound to obey; by which means they come again to be out of subjection and may constitute to themselves a *new legislative,* as they think best, being in full liberty to resist the force of those who without authority would impose anything upon them. Everyone is at the disposure of his own will when those who had, by the delegation of the society, the declaring of the public will are excluded from it and others usurp the place who have no such authority or delegation.

§. 213. This being usually brought about by such in the commonwealth who misuse the power they have, it is hard to consider it aright and know at whose door to lay it without knowing the form of government in which it happens. Let us suppose then the legislative placed in the concurrence of three distinct persons:

1. A single hereditary person having the constant, supreme, executive power, and with it the power of convoking and dissolving the other two within certain periods of time.
2. An assembly of hereditary nobility.
3. An assembly of representatives chosen, *pro tempore,* by the people. Such a form of government supposed, it is evident:°

§. 214. *First,* that when such a single person or prince sets up his own arbitrary will in place of the laws, which are the will of the society declared by the legislative, then the *legislative is changed.* For that being in effect the legislative whose rules and laws are put in execution and required to be obeyed, when other laws are set up and other rules pretended and enforced than what the legislative, constituted by the society, have enacted, it is plain that the *legislative is changed*. Whoever introduces new laws, not being thereunto authorized by the fundamental appointment of the society, or subverts the old, disowns and overturns the power by which they were made and so sets up a *new legislative*.

§. 215. *Secondly,* when the prince hinders the legislative from assembling in its due time or from acting freely, pursuant to those ends for which it was constituted, the *legislative is altered*. For it is not a certain number of men, no, nor their meeting, unless they have also freedom of debating and leisure of perfecting what is for the good of the society, wherein the legislative consists. When these are taken away or altered, so as to deprive the society of the due exercise of their power, the *legislative* is truly altered. For it is not names that constitute governments, but the use and exercise of those powers that were intended to accompany them. So that he who takes away the freedom or hinders the acting of the legislative in its due seasons, in effect, takes *away the legislative* and *puts an end to the government*.

§. 216. *Thirdly,* when, by the arbitrary power of the prince, the electors or ways of election are altered without the consent and contrary to the common interest of the people, there also the *legislative is altered*. For if others than those whom the society hath authorized thereunto do choose, or in another way than what the society hath prescribed, those chosen are not the legislative appointed by the people.

§. 217. *Fourthly,* the delivery also of the people into the subjection of a foreign power, either by the prince or by the legislative, is certainly a *change of the legislative* and so a *dissolution of the government*. For the end why people entered into society being to be preserved one entire, free, independent society, to be governed by its own laws, this is lost, whenever they are given up into the power of another.

§. 218. Why, in such a constitution as this, the *dissolution of the government* in these cases is to be imputed to the prince is evident: because he, having the force, treasure and offices of the state to employ, and often persuading himself or being flattered by others that as supreme magistrate he is incapable of control, he alone is in a condition to make great advances toward such changes under pretence of lawful authority, and has it in his hands to terrify or suppress opposers, as factious, seditious, and enemies to the government. Whereas no other part of the legislative or people is capable by themselves to attempt any alteration of the legislative without open and visible rebellion, apt enough to be taken notice of, which, when it prevails, produces effects very little different from foreign conquest. Besides, the prince in such a form of government, having the power of dissolving the other parts of the legislative and thereby rendering them private persons, they can never in opposition to him or without his concurrence alter the legislative by a law, his consent being necessary to give any of their decrees that sanction. But yet, so far as the other parts of the legislative any way contribute to any attempt upon the government, and do either promote or not, what lies in them, hinder such designs, they are guilty and partake in this, which is certainly the greatest crime men can be guilty of one towards another.

§. 219. There is one way more whereby such a government may be dissolved, and that is when he who has the supreme executive power neglects and abandons that charge, so that the laws already made can no longer be put in execution. This is demonstratively to reduce all to anarchy and so effectually *to dissolve the government*. For laws not being made for themselves, but to be, by their execution, the bonds of the society, to keep every part of the body politic in its due place and function, when that totally ceases, the *government* visibly *ceases* and the people become a confused multitude without order or connection. Where there is no longer the administration of justice for the securing of men's rights, nor any remaining power within the community to direct the force or provide for the necessities of the public, there certainly is *no government left*. Where the laws cannot be executed, it is all one as if there were no laws; and a government without laws is, I suppose, a mystery in politics, inconceivable to human capacity and inconsistent with human society.

§. 220. In these and the like cases, *when the government is dissolved* the people are at liberty to provide for themselves by erecting a new legislative, differing from the other by the change of persons or form or both, as they shall find it most for their safety and good. For the *society* can never, by the fault of another, lose the native and original right it has to preserve itself, which can only be done by a settled legislative and a fair and impartial execution of the laws made by it. But the state of mankind is not so miserable that they are not capable of using this remedy until it be too late to look for any. To tell *people* they *may provide for themselves* by erecting a new legislative, when by oppression, artifice, or being delivered over to a foreign power their old one is gone, is only to tell them they may expect relief when it is too late and the evil is past cure. This is in effect no more than to bid them first be slaves and then to take care of their liberty, and when their chains are on tell them they may act like freemen. This, if barely so, is rather mockery than relief. And men can never be secure from tyranny, if there be no means to escape it until they are perfectly under it; and therefore it is that they have not only a right to get out of it, but to prevent it.

§. 221. There is therefore, secondly, another way whereby *governments are dissolved,* and that is when the legislative or the prince, either of them, act contrary to their trust.

First, the *legislative acts against the trust* reposed in them when they endeavour to invade the property of the subject and to make themselves, or any part of the community, masters or arbitrary disposers of the lives, liberties, or fortunes of the people.

§. 222. The reason why men enter into society is the preservation of their property; and the end why they choose and authorize a legislative is that there may be laws made and rules set, as guards and fences to the properties of all the members of the society, to limit the power and moderate the dominion of every part and member of the society. For since it can never be supposed to be the will of the society that the legislative should have a power to destroy that which everyone designs to secure by entering into society, and for which the people submitted themselves to legislators of their own making, whenever the *legislators endeavour to take away and destroy the property of the people,* or to reduce them to slavery under arbitrary power, they put themselves into a state of war with the people, who are thereupon absolved from any farther obedience and are left to the common refuge which God hath provided for all men against force and violence. Whensoever therefore the *legislative* shall transgress this fundamental rule of society and either by ambition, fear, folly or corruption *endeavour to grasp* themselves *or put into the hands of any other an absolute power* over the lives, liberties, and estates of the people, by this breach of trust they forfeit *the power* the people had put into their hands for quite contrary ends, and it devolves to the people, who have a right to resume their original liberty and, by the establishment of a new legislative (such as they shall think fit), provide for their own safety and security, which is the end for which they are in society. What I have said here concerning the legislative in general holds true also concerning the supreme executor, who, having a double trust put in him, both to have a part in the legislative and the supreme execution of the law, acts against both when he goes about to set up his own arbitrary will as the law of the society. He *acts* also *contrary to his trust* when he either employs the force, treasure, and offices of the society to corrupt the *representatives* and gain them to his purposes, or openly preengages the *electors* and prescribes to their choice such whom he has, by solicitations, threats, promises, or otherwise, won to his designs, and employs them to bring in such who have promised beforehand what to vote and what to enact. Thus to regulate candidates and electors and new-model the ways of election, what is it but to cut up the government by the roots and poison the very fountain of public security? For the people, having reserved to themselves the choice of their *representatives* as the fence to their properties, could do it for no other end but that they might always be freely chosen, and so chosen, freely act and advise, as the necessity of the commonwealth and the public good should, upon examination and mature debate, be judged to require. This, those who give their votes before they hear the debate and have weighed the reasons on all sides, are not capable of doing. To prepare such an assembly as this and endeavour to set up the declared abettors of his own will for the true *representatives* of the people and the law-makers of the society, is certainly as great a *breach of trust* and as perfect a declaration of a design to subvert the government as is possible to be met with. To which, if one shall add rewards and punishments visibly employed to the same end and all the arts of perverted law made use of to take off and destroy all that stand in the way of such a design and will not comply and consent to betray the liberties of their country, it will be past doubt what is doing. What power they ought to have in the society who thus employ it contrary to the trust that went along with it in its first institution, is easy to determine; and one cannot but see that he who has once attempted any such thing as this cannot any longer be trusted.

§. 223. To this perhaps it will be said that the people being ignorant and always discontented, to lay the foundation of government in the unsteady opinion and uncertain humour of the people is to expose it to certain ruin.° And *no government will be able long to subsist* if the people may set up a new legislative whenever they take offence at the old one. To this I answer: quite the contrary. People are not so easily got out of their old forms as some are apt to suggest. They are hardly to be prevailed with to amend the acknowledged faults in the frame they have been accustomed to. And if there be any original defects or adventitious ones introduced by time or corruption, it is not an easy thing to get them changed, even when all the world sees there is an opportunity for it. This slowness and aversion in the people to quit their old constitutions has, in the many revolutions which have been seen in this kingdom in this and former ages, still kept us to or, after some interval of fruitless attempts, still brought us back again to our old legislative of king, lords and commons. And whatever provocations have made the crown be taken from some of our princes' heads, they never carried the people so far as to place it in another line.

§. 224. But it will be said, this *hypothesis* lays a *ferment for* frequent *rebellion*. To which I answer:

First, no more than any other *hypothesis.* For when the people are made miserable and find themselves *exposed to the ill usage of arbitrary power,* cry up their governors as much as you will for sons of *Jupiter,* let them be sacred and divine, descended or authorized from heaven, give them out for whom or what you please, the same will happen. *The people generally ill-treated* and contrary to right will be ready upon any occasion to ease themselves of a burden that sits heavy upon them. They will wish and seek for the opportunity which, in the change, weakness and accidents of human affairs, seldom delays long to offer itself. He must have lived but a little while in the world who has not seen examples of this in his time; and he must have read very little who cannot produce examples of it in all sorts of governments in the world.

§. 225. *Secondly,* I answer, such *revolutions happen* not upon every little mismanagement in public affairs. *Great mistakes* in the ruling part, many wrong and inconvenient laws, and all the *slips* of human frailty will be *borne by the people* without mutiny or murmur. But if a long train of abuses, prevarications and artifices, all tending the same way, make the design visible to the people, and they cannot but feel what they lie under and see whither they are going, it is not to be wondered that they should then rouse themselves and endeavour to put the rule into such hands which may secure to them the ends for which government was at first erected; and, without which, ancient names and specious forms are so far from being better, that they are much worse than the state of nature or pure anarchy, the inconveniencies being all as great and as near, but the remedy farther off and more difficult.

§. 226. *Thirdly,* I answer, that *this doctrine* of a power in the people of providing for their safety anew by a new legislative, when their legislators have acted contrary to their trust by invading their property, is *the best fence against rebellion* and the probablest means to hinder it. For *rebellion* being an opposition not to persons but authority, which is founded only in the constitutions and laws of the government, those, whoever they be, who by force break through and by force justify their violation of them, are truly and properly *rebels*. For when men, by entering into society and civil government, have excluded force and introduced laws for the preservation of property, peace, and unity amongst themselves, those who set up force again in opposition to the laws do *rebellare,* that is, bring back again the state of war, and are properly rebels; which they who are in power (by the pretence they have to authority, the temptation of force they have in their hands, and the flattery of those about them), being likeliest to do, the properest way to prevent the evil is to show them the danger and injustice of it who are under the greatest temptation to run into it.

§. 227. In both the aforementioned cases, when either the legislative is changed or the legislators act contrary to the end for which they were constituted, those who are guilty are *guilty of rebellion*. For if anyone by force takes away the established legislative of any society and the laws by them made pursuant to their trust, he thereby takes away the umpirage which everyone had consented to for a peaceable decision of all their controversies and a bar to the state of war amongst them. They who remove or change the legislative take away this decisive power, which nobody can have but by the appointment and consent of the people. And so destroying the authority which the people did, and nobody else can, set up, and introducing a power which the people hath not authorized, they actually *introduce a state of war,* which is that of force without authority. And thus, by removing the legislative established by the society (in whose decisions the people acquiesced and united, as to that of their own will), they untie the knot and *expose the people anew to the state of war.* And if those who by force take away the legislative are *rebels,* the *legislators* themselves, as has been shown, can be no less esteemed so when they, who were set up for the protection and preservation of the people, their liberties and properties, shall by force invade and endeavour to take them away. And so they, putting themselves into a state of war with those who made them the protectors and guardians of their peace, are properly, and with the greatest aggravation, *rebellantes,* rebels.

§. 228. But if they who say *it lays a foundation for rebellion* mean that it may occasion civil wars or intestine broils to tell the people they are absolved from obedience when illegal attempts are made upon their liberties or properties, and may oppose the unlawful violence of those who were their magistrates when they invade their properties contrary to the trust put in them, and that therefore this doctrine is not to be allowed, being so destructive to the peace of the world: they may as well say, upon the same ground, that honest men may not oppose robbers or pirates because this may occasion disorder or bloodshed. If any *mischief* come in such cases, it is not to be charged upon him who defends his own right, but *on him that invades* his neighbour's. If the innocent honest man must quietly quit all he has, for peace sake, to him who will lay violent hands upon it, I desire it may be considered what a kind of peace there will be in the world which consists only in violence and rapine and which is to be maintained only for the benefit of robbers and oppressors. Who would not think it an admirable peace between the mighty and the mean when the lamb, without resistance, yielded his throat to be torn by the imperious wolf? *Polyphemus*'s den gives us a perfect pattern of such a peace and such a government, wherein *Ulysses* and his companions had nothing to do but quietly to suffer themselves to be devoured. And no doubt *Ulysses*, who was a prudent man, preached up *passive obedience* and exhorted them to a quiet submission, by representing to them of what concernment peace was to mankind, and by showing the inconveniencies might happen if they should offer to resist *Polyphemus*, who had now the power over them.

§. 229. The end of government is the good of mankind. And which is *best for mankind:* that the people should be always exposed to the boundless will of tyranny, or that the rulers should be sometimes liable to be opposed, when they grow exorbitant in the use of their power and employ it for the destruction, and not the preservation, of the properties of their people?

§. 230. Nor let anyone say that mischief can arise from hence, as often as it shall please a busy head or turbulent spirit to desire the alteration of the government. It is true, such men may stir, whenever they please; but it will be only to their own just ruin and perdition. For until the mischief be grown general and the ill designs of the rulers become visible or their attempts sensible to the greater part, the people, who are more disposed to suffer than right themselves by resistance, are not apt to stir. The examples of particular injustice or oppression of here and there an unfortunate man moves them not. But if they universally have a persuasion, grounded upon manifest evidence, that designs are carrying on against their liberties, and the general course and tendency of things cannot but give them strong suspicions of the evil intention of their governors, who is to be blamed for it? Who can help it if they, who might avoid it, bring themselves into this suspicion? Are the people to be blamed if they have the sense of rational creatures and can think of things no otherwise than as they find and feel them? And is it not rather *their fault* who put things into such a posture, that they would not have them thought to be as they are? I grant that the pride, ambition, and turbulency of private men have sometimes caused great disorders in commonwealths, and factions have been fatal to states and kingdoms. But whether *the mischief* hath *oftener* begun *in the people's wantonness* and a desire to cast off the lawful authority of their rulers, or *in the rulers' insolence* and endeavours to get and exercise an arbitrary power over their people, whether oppression or disobedience gave the first rise to the disorder, I leave it to impartial history to determine. This I am sure: whoever, either ruler or subject, by force goes about to invade the rights of either prince or people and lays the foundation for *overturning* the constitution and frame of *any just government,* is highly guilty of the greatest crime, I think, a man is capable of, being to answer for all those mischiefs of blood, rapine, and desolation which the breaking to pieces of governments bring on a country. And he who does it is justly to be esteemed the common enemy and pest of mankind and is to be treated accordingly.

§. 231. That *subjects* or *foreigners,* attempting by force on the properties of any people, may be *resisted* with force is agreed on all hands. But that *magistrates,* doing the same thing, may be *resisted* hath of late been denied: as if those who had the greatest privileges and advantages by the law had thereby a power to break those laws, by which alone they were set in a better place than their brethren. Whereas their offence is thereby the greater, both as being ungrateful for the greater share they have by the law and breaking also that trust which is put into their hands by their brethren.

§. 232. Whosoever uses *force without right,* as everyone does in society who does it without law, puts himself into a *state of war* with those against whom he so uses it; and in that state all former ties are cancelled, all other rights cease, and everyone has a right to defend himself and *to resist the aggressor.* This is so evident that *Barclay* himself, that great assertor of the power and sacredness of kings, is forced to confess that it is lawful for the people, in some cases, to *resist* their king; and that too in a chapter wherein he pretends to show that the divine law shuts up the people from all manner of rebellion. Whereby it is evident, even by his own doctrine, that since they may in some cases *resist,* all resisting of *princes* is not rebellion. His words are these. *Quod siquis dicat, Ergone populus tyrannicæ crudelitati & furori jugulum semper præbehit? Ergone multitudo civitates suas fame, ferro, & flammâ vastari, seque, conjuges, & liberos fortunæ ludibrio & tyranni libidini exponi, inque omnia vitæ pericula omnesque miserias & molestias á rege deduci patientur? Num illis quod omni animantium generi est á naturâ tributum, denegari debet, ut sc. vim vi repellant, seseq; ab injuriâ tueantur? Huic breviter responsum sit, Populo universo negari defensionem, quæ juris naturalis est, neque ultionem quæ præter naturam est adversus regem concedi debere. Quapropter si rex non in singulares tantum personas aliquot privatum odium exerceat, sed corpus etiam reipublicæ, cujus ipse caput est, i. e. totum populum, vel insignem aliquam ejus partem immani & intolerandâ seu tyrannide divexet; populo, quidem hoc casu resistendi ac tuendi se ab injuriâ potestas competit, sed tuendi se tantum, non enim in principem invadendi: & restituendæ injuriæ illatæ, non recedendi à debitâ reverentiâ propter acceptam injuriam. Præsentem denique impetum propul-*

*sandi non vim præteritam ulciscenti jus habet. Horum
enim alterum à naturâ est, ut vitam scilicet corpusque
tueamur. Alterum vero contra naturam, ut inferior de
superiori supplicium sumat. Quod itaque populus malum,
antequam factum sit, impedire potest, ne fiat, id postquam
factum est, in regem authorem sceleris vindicare non
potest: populus igitur hoc ampliùs quam privatus quispiam
habet: quod huic, vel ipsis adversariis judicibus, excepto
Buchanano, nullum nisi in patientia remedium superest.
Cùm ille si intolerabilis tyrannus est (modicum enim ferre
omnino debet) resistere cum reverentiâ possit,* Barclay
contra Monarchom. l. iii. c. 8.

In English thus:

§. 233. *But if anyone should ask, must the people then
always lay themselves open to the cruelty and rage of tyranny? Must they see their cities pillaged, and laid in ashes,
their wives and children exposed to the tyrant's lust and
fury, and themselves and families reduced by their king to
ruin and all the miseries of want and oppression, and yet
sit still? Must men alone be debarred the common privilege
of opposing force with force, which nature allows so freely
to all other creatures for their preservation from injury? I
answer: self-defence is a part of the law of nature, nor can
it be denied the community, even against the king himself;
but to revenge themselves upon him must by no means be
allowed them, it being not agreeable to that law. Wherefore if the king shall show an hatred, not only to some particular persons, but sets himself against the body of the
commonwealth, whereof he is the head, and shall, with
intolerable ill usage, cruelly tyrannize over the whole or a
considerable part of the people, in this case the people have
a right to resist and defend themselves from injury; but it
must be with this caution, that they only defend themselves but do not attack their prince. They may repair the
damages received, but must not for any provocation exceed*

the bounds of due reverence and respect. They may repulse
the present attempt, but must not revenge past violences.
For it is natural for us to defend life and limb, but that an
inferior should punish a superior is against nature. The
mischief which is designed them the people may prevent
before it be done; but when it is done, they must not
revenge it on the king, though author of the villainy. This
therefore is the privilege of the people in general, above
what any private person hath: that particular men are
allowed by our adversaries themselves (Buchanan only
excepted) to have no other remedy but patience, but the
body of the people may with respect resist intolerable tyr-
anny. For when it is but moderate, they ought to endure it.

§. 234. Thus far that great advocate of monarchical power
allows of *resistance*.

§. 235. It is true, he has annexed two limitations to it, to
no purpose:
　　First, he says, it must be with reverence.
　　Secondly, it must be without retribution or punishment. And the reason he gives is *because an inferior can-*
not punish a superior.
　　First, how to *resist force without striking again,* or
how to *strike with reverence,* will need some skill to make
intelligible. He that shall oppose an assault only with a
shield to receive the blows, or in any more respectful posture, without a sword in his hand to abate the confidence
and force of the assailant, will quickly be at an end of his
resistance and will find such a defence serve only to draw
on himself the worse usage. This is as ridiculous a way of
resisting as *Juvenal* thought it of fighting: *ubi tu pulsas,*
ego vapulo tantum. And the success of the combat will be
unavoidably the same he there describes it:

—Libertas pauperis hæc est:
Pulsatus rogat, & pugnis concisus, adorat,
Ut liceat paucis cum dentibus inde reverti.

This will always be the event of such an imaginary *resistance,* where men may not strike again. He therefore *who may resist must be allowed to strike.* And then let our author, or anybody else, join a knock on the head or a cut on the face with as much *reverence* and *respect* as he thinks fit. He that can reconcile blows and reverence, may, for aught I know, desire for his pains a civil, respectful cudgeling wherever he can meet with it.

Secondly, as to his second, *an inferior cannot punish a superior:* that is true, generally speaking, whilst he is his superior. But to resist force with force, being *the state of war* that *levels the parties,* cancels all former relation of reverence, respect, and *superiority.* And then the odds that remains is that he who opposes the unjust aggressor has this *superiority* over him, that he has a right, when he prevails, to punish the offender, both for the breach of the peace and all the evils that followed upon it. *Barclay* therefore, in another place, more coherently to himself denies it to be lawful to *resist* a king in any case. But he there assigns two cases whereby a king may un-king himself. His words are, *Quid ergo, nulline casus incidere possunt quibus populo sese erigere atque in regem impotentius dominantem arma capere & invadere jure suo suâque authoritate liceat? Nulli certe quamdiu rex manet. Semper enim ex divinis id obstat, Regem honorificato; & qui potestati resistit, Dei ordinationi resistit: non aliàs igitur in eum populo potestas est quam si id committat propter quod ipso jure rex esse desinat. Tunc enim se ipse principatu exuit atque in privatis constituit liber: hoc modo populus & superior efficitur, reverso ad eum sc. jure illo quod ante regem inauguratum in interregno habuit.*

At sunt paucorum generum commissa ejusmodi quæ hunc
effectum pariunt. At ego cum plurima animo perlustrem,
duo tantum invenio, duos, inquam, casus quibus rex ipso
facto ex rege non regem se facit & omni honore & dignitate
regali atque in subditos potestate destituit; quorum etiam
meminit Winzerus. Horum unus est, Si regnum disperdat,
quemadmodum de Nerone fertur, quod is nempe senatum
populumque Romanum, atque adeo urbem ipsam ferro
flammaque vastare, ac novas sibi sedes quærere decrevis-
set. Et de Caligula, quod palam denunciarit se neque
civem neque principem senatui amplius fore, inque animo
habuerit interempto utriusque ordinis electissimo quoque
Alexandriam commigrare, ac ut populum uno ictu interi-
meret, unam ei cervicem optavit. Talia cum rex aliquis
meditatur & molitur serio, omnem regnandi curam & ani-
mum ilico abjicit, ac proinde imperium in subditos amit-
tit, ut dominus servi pro derelicto habiti dominium.

§. 236. *Alter casus est, Si rex in alicujus clientelam se con-*
tulit; ac regnum quod liberum à majoribus & populo tra-
ditum accepit, alienæ ditioni mancipavit. Nam tunc
quamvis forte non eâ mente id agit populo plane ut incom-
modet: tamen quia quod præcipuum est regiæ dignitatis
amisit, ut summus scilicet in regno secundum Deum sit, &
solo Deo inferior, atque populum etiam totum ignorantem
vel invitum, cujus libertatem sartam & tectam conservare
debuit, in alterius gentis ditionem & potestatem dedidit;
hâc velut quadam regni ab alienatione effecit, ut nec quod
ipse in regno imperium habuit retineat, nec in eum cui col-
latum voluit, juris quicquam transferat; atque ita eo facto
liberum jam & suæ potestatis populum relinquit, cujus rei
exemplum unum annales Scotici suppeditant. Barclay
contra Monarchom. l. iii. c. 16.

Which in *English* runs thus:

§. 237. *What then, can there no case happen wherein the people may of right and by their own authority help themselves, take arms, and set upon their king, imperiously domineering over them? None at all, whilst he remains a king. Honour the king, and he that resists the power, resists the ordinance of God, are divine oracles that will never permit it. The people therefore can never come by a power over him, unless he does something that makes him cease to be a king. For then he divests himself of his crown and dignity and returns to the state of a private man, and the people become free and superior, the power which they had in the interregnum, before they crowned him king devolving to them again. But there are but few miscarriages which bring the matter to this state. After considering it well on all sides, I can find but two. Two cases there are, I say, whereby a king, ipso facto, becomes no king and loses all power and regal authority over his people; which are also taken notice of by Winzerus. The first is, If he endeavour to overturn the government, that is, if he have a purpose and design to ruin the kingdom and commonwealth, as it is recorded of Nero that he resolved to cut off the senate and people of Rome, lay the city waste with fire and sword, and then remove to some other place. And of Caligula, that he openly declared that he would be no longer a head to the people or senate, and that he had it in his thoughts to cut off the worthiest men of both ranks and then retire to Alexandria; and he wished that the people had but one neck, that he might dispatch them all at a blow. Such designs as these, when any king harbours in his thoughts and seriously promotes, he immediately gives up all care and thought of the commonwealth, and consequently forfeits the power of governing his subjects, as a master does the dominion over his slaves whom he hath abandoned.*

§. 238. *The other case is, When a king makes himself the dependent of another and subjects his kingdom which his ancestors left him and the people put free into his hands, to the dominion of another. For however perhaps it may not be his intention to prejudice the people, yet because he has hereby lost the principal part of regal dignity, viz. to be next and immediately under God, supreme in his kingdom, and also because he betrayed or forced his people, whose liberty he ought to have carefully preserved, into the power and dominion of a foreign nation. By this, as it were, alienation of his kingdom, he himself loses the power he had in it before, without transferring any the least right to those on whom he would have bestowed it; and so by this act sets the people free and leaves them at their own disposal. One example of this is to be found in the Scotch Annals.*

§. 239. In these cases *Barclay,* the great champion of absolute monarchy, is forced to allow that a king may be *resisted* and *ceases to be a king.* That is, in short, not to multiply cases, in whatsoever he has *no authority,* there he is *no king* and may be *resisted.* For wheresoever the *authority ceases, the king ceases too,* and becomes like other men who have no authority. And these two cases he instances in, differ little from those above mentioned to be destructive to governments, only that he has omitted the principle from which his doctrine flows: and that is the breach of trust in not preserving the form of government agreed on and in not intending the end of government itself, which is the public good and preservation of property. When a king has dethroned himself and put himself in a state of war with his people, what shall hinder them from prosecuting him, who is no king, as they would any other man who has put himself into state of war with them? *Barclay,* and those of his opinion, would do well to tell us.° This farther I desire may be taken notice of out of

Barclay, that he says, *The mischief that is designed them the people may prevent before it be done,* whereby he allows *resistance* when tyranny is but in design. *Such designs as these* (says he), *when any king harbours in his thoughts and seriously promotes, he immediately gives up all care and thought of the commonwealth,* so that, according to him, the neglect of the public good is to be taken as an evidence of such *design,* or at least for a sufficient cause of *resistance.* And the reason of all he gives in these words, *because he betrayed or forced his people, whose liberty he ought carefully to have preserved.* What he adds, *into the power and dominion of a foreign nation,* signifies nothing, the fault and forfeiture lying in the loss of their *liberty,* which he *ought to have preserved,* and not in any distinction of the persons to whose dominion they were subjected. The people's right is equally invaded and their liberty lost whether they are made slaves to any of their own or a *foreign nation;* and in this lies the injury and against this only have they the right of defence. And there are instances to be found in all countries which show that it is not the change of nations in the persons of their governors, but the change of government, that gives the offence. *Bilson,* a bishop of our church and a great stickler for the power and prerogative of princes, does, if I mistake not, in his treatise of *Christian subjection,* acknowledge that *princes may forfeit their power* and their title to the obedience of their subjects; and if there needed authority in a case where reason is so plain, I could send my reader to *Bracton, Fortescue,* and the author of *the Mirrour,* and others, writers that cannot be suspected to be ignorant of our government or enemies to it. But I thought *Hooker* alone might be enough to satisfy those men who, relying on him for their ecclesiastical polity, are by a strange fate carried to deny those principles upon which he builds it. Whether they are herein made the tools of more cunning workmen, to pull down their own fabric, they were best look. This I am sure, their civil policy is so new, so dangerous, and so destructive to both rulers and people that as former ages never could bear the broaching of it; so it may be hoped, those to come, redeemed from the impositions of these *Egyptian* under-taskmasters, will abhor the memory of such servile flatterers, who, whilst it seemed to serve their turn, resolved all government into absolute tyranny and would have all men born to, what their mean souls fitted them for, slavery.

§. 240. Here, it is like, the common question will be made, *Who shall be judge* whether the prince or legislative act contrary to their trust? This, perhaps, ill-affected and factious men may spread amongst the people, when the prince only makes use of his due prerogative. To this I reply, *The people shall be judge;* for who shall be *judge* whether his trustee or deputy acts well and according to the trust reposed in him, but he who deputes him, and must, by having deputed him, have still a power to discard him when he fails in his trust?° If this be reasonable in particular cases of private men, why should it be otherwise in that of the greatest moment, where the welfare of millions is concerned, and also where the evil, if not prevented, is greater and the redress very difficult, dear, and dangerous?

§. 241. But farther, this question, *(Who shall be judge?)* cannot mean that there is no judge at all. For where there is no judicature on earth to decide controversies amongst men, *God* in heaven is *judge.* He alone, it is true, is judge of the right. But *every man* is *judge* for himself, as in all other cases, so in this, whether another hath put himself into a state of war with him and whether he should appeal to the Supreme Judge, as *Jephtha* did.

§. 242. If a controversy arise between a prince and some of the people, in a matter where the law is silent or doubtful and the thing be of great consequence, I should think the proper *umpire,* in such a case, should be the body of the *people.* For in cases where the prince hath a trust reposed in him and is dispensed from the common ordinary rules of the law, there, if any men find themselves aggrieved and think the prince acts contrary to or beyond that trust, who so proper to *judge* as the body of the *people* (who, at first, lodged that trust in him), how far they meant it should extend? But if the prince, or whoever they be in the administration, decline that way of determination, the appeal then lies nowhere but to heaven, force between either persons who have no known superior on earth, or which permits no appeal to a judge on earth, being properly a state of war wherein the appeal lies only to heaven. And in that state the *injured party must judge* for himself when he will think fit to make use of that appeal and put himself upon it.

§. 243. To conclude, The *power that every individual gave the society* when he entered into it can never revert to the individuals again, as long as the society lasts, but will always remain in the community; because without this there can be no community, no commonwealth, which is contrary to the original agreement. So also when the society hath placed the legislative in any assembly of men to continue in them and their successors, with direction and authority for providing such successors, *the legislative can never revert to the people* whilst that government lasts; because having provided a legislative with power to continue forever, they have given up their political power to the legislative and cannot resume it. But if they have set limits to the duration of their legislative, and made this supreme power in any person or assembly only temporary, or else, when by the miscarriages of those in authority it is forfeited: upon the forfeiture, or at the determination of the time set, *it reverts to the society,* and the people have a right to act as supreme and continue the legislative in themselves, or erect a new form, or under the old form place it in new hands, as they think good.

FINIS.

Notes

p. 7 *saved the nation when it was on the very brink of slavery and ruin*:
William III (Prince of Orange) ruled England, Ireland, and Scot-
land from 1689 until his death in 1702 (ruling with his wife, Queen
Mary II, until her death in 1694). His invasion of England in 1688
initiated the "Glorious Revolution" that led to James II being
deposed and subsequently "vacating" the throne by fleeing to
France. William's claim to the throne was through his mother,
Charles I's daughter, and his wife (and cousin) Mary, daughter of
the Duke of York (later James II). William was the leader of a Prot-
estant alliance opposing Catholic France, and he feared that a
Catholic king on England's throne would result in a powerful
union with France.

CHAPTER I

p. 12 *than what Sir* Robert Filmer *hath taught us*: This section is
designed to summarize Locke's refutation of Filmer in the *First
Treatise of Government*. Robert Filmer (1588–1653), knighted by
James I, was a steadfast supporter of the absolute authority and

divine right of kings, basing his views in a "patriarchalist" account of the paternal authority of Adam being passed down to contemporary monarchs. A posthumous publication of some of Filmer's works in 1679–80 revived their popularity among royalists and inspired Locke's lengthy attacks.

CHAPTER II

p. 14 *This* equality *of men by nature, the judicious* Hooker: Richard Hooker (1554–1600), a widely respected priest and theologian in the Church of England, was often taken as an authority by some of those Locke is writing against. Hooker's principal work was *Of the Laws of Ecclesiastical Polity*, and this is the first of 16 quotations from that work that Locke inserted into the text of the *Second Treatise* (in order "to satisfy those" rivals [§239]).

p. 15 *his property whose workmanship they are*: Compare Locke's claim here that humans are God's property with his later apparent claims that persons own themselves (§§27, 44).

p. 15 *as much as he can,* to preserve the rest of mankind: When combined with §42 of the *First Treatise*, this passage makes it clear that any strict libertarian reading of Locke's moral theory, according to which there are no positive moral duties to assist others, must fail.

p. 15 *punish the transgressors of that law to such a degree as may hinder its violation*: Locke mentions both deterrence-based and retributivist standards for just punishment in the state of nature. Here he suggests deterrence: wrongdoers may be punished "to such a degree as may hinder" violation of the law of nature; but immediately after, in §8, he writes that punishment should "retribute" to an offender "what is proportionate to his transgression." Locke then follows this by again asserting that punishment should be for "reparation and restraint," to "thereby deter him, and by his example others." §12 also suggests deterrence-based standards.

p. 16 *I doubt not but this will seem a very strange doctrine to some men*: Locke's referring to his position as a "very strange doctrine" may indicate that he thinks of it as novel or original. In fact, both the doctrine and Locke's principal argument for it can be found in Hugo Grotius (*De Jure Praedae Commentarius*, 8).

p. 18 *has a right to demand in his own name, and he alone can remit*: The distinction here between the right of "punishing the crime for restraint" and the right of "taking reparation" for injury provides a moral basis for the distinction between the roles of criminal and civil (or private) law. Locke appears to suggest that the latter right of taking reparation cannot be surrendered to "the magistrate," so that a legal system that denied injured parties the right to take reparation from a wrongdoer would be violating an inalienable natural right.

p. 19 *a studier of that law as the positive laws of the commonwealths*: Locke's claims here that the law of nature is "intelligible and plain to a rational creature" suggest that this moral law is capable of easy rational demonstration. There is, however, nothing in the *Two Treatises* that helps us to understand how such a demonstration would proceed. We know that by the time Locke wrote *The Reasonableness of Christianity* (published in 1695), he had more or less given up on the project of producing such a demonstration (although even there, contrary to common claims, Locke never says that such a demonstration is impossible or that no *parts* of natural law had ever actually been successfully demonstrated).

CHAPTER III

p. 23 *and so be looked on as* in a state of war: The closing lines of this section are an initial attempt to accuse Kings Charles and James of having initiated a state of war with the people of England, thus justifying forceful popular resistance to and punishment of the Stuart monarchs. That theme is repeatedly emphasized later in the text.

CHAPTER IV

p. 27 *Freedom then is not what* Sir Robert Filmer *tells us,* Observations, A. *55*: This is the only mention of any of Filmer's specific works in the *Second Treatise*. The bulk of this text, unlike Locke's *First Treatise*, rarely even mentions Filmer by name while criticizing his views.

p. 28 *arbitrary power of another, to take away his life when he pleases*: Locke's remarks here are often characterized as a defense of the kinds of inalienable rights recognized by modern legal systems (such as the legal right not to be a slave, a right we cannot surrender). Locke in fact says not that we have rights over ourselves that we cannot alienate, but rather only that one "cannot give more power than he has himself." Our rights over ourselves are limited from the start. There is a difference between saying that I own this book, but cannot sell it, and saying that I don't own this book in the first place.

p. 29 *but the loss of an eye, or tooth, set him free,* Exod. *xxi*: Locke's distinction here between slavery and "drudgery" implies that even very onerous contracts—such as contracts into indentured servitude—can be morally binding, since they do not permit the masters to kill their servants and they expire after a period of time. Contracts into chattel slavery, by contrast, are not binding, being limitless (specifically, with respect to life and freedom). Such contracts would involve contracting away something we do not possess.

CHAPTER V

p. 30 Adam *and his heirs in succession, exclusive of all the rest of his posterity*: The wording here (along with Locke's summary of his argument in §39) makes it clear that Locke's target in the chapter is Filmer's inferences from God's gift to Adam. By beginning instead with the idea that God gave the earth "to mankind in common," Locke poses for himself the great natural-law puzzle about property: how could persons come to have exclusive, private property "in several parts" of the earth, without it constituting an injury to the other "commoners"? It is important to notice that "property" in this chapter is being used in its familiar, narrow sense—that is, a right over external goods (or "estate"). Locke later also uses a broader notion of "property," where the term refers to anything to which we have a right, including our lives and liberties (see §§87, 123).

p. 31 *joined it to something that is his own, and thereby makes it his property*: This is Locke's famous and controversial "labor-mixing" account of natural property rights (reiterated in §44). Locke is writing here about the "initial acquisition" of natural property rights—that is, about how one can (in a state of nature) make something previously unowned (or owned only in common with others) into something privately owned. Once private ownership is established in this way, owned objects can, of course, subsequently come to be owned by others in different ways than by laboring on them (such as purchase, gift, inheritance, etc.).

p. 32 *and as good, left in common for others*: Here Locke first states (and then repeats in §33) what Robert Nozick called "the Lockean Proviso"—namely, the requirement on initial acquisition that there be "enough and as good left in common for others." The motivation appears to be that appropriations that respect this proviso cannot be "any prejudice to any other man" (§33), cannot be fairly counted as an "injury" to anyone (§36).

p. 32 *And so they became his private right*: As promised in §25, Locke argues here that his labor-mixing argument (presumably, when combined with the "enough and as good" proviso) obviates the need to obtain universal consent (given by all of the other people to whom the earth was given in common by God) prior to making private property in a share of the common earth. This universal-consent requirement operates centrally not only in Filmer, but in Grotius and Pufendorf as well. Locke also suggests here that a requirement of universal consent could not have been part of God's plan for his gift to mankind, since if it had been, "man had starved" while waiting to obtain consent from everyone.

p. 34 *Whatever is beyond this is more than his share and belongs to others*: This is the first statement of what at least appears to be a second "proviso" or limit on initial acquisition—a requirement that we appropriate only what we can use "before it spoils." Locke would, I believe, say the same of any wasting of natural goods, even if it does not involve spoilage (but only, say, appropriating and then concealing or destroying useful things). Locke's later statement of this limit on appropriation of unowned natural goods says that one's appropriation is permissible "so long as nothing perished uselessly in his hands" (§46).

p. 37 *how it has done, I shall by and by show more at large*: Locke argues here that the "tacit agreement of men to put a value on" money gives some people "a right" to "larger possessions" than would otherwise be permissible. He continues this argument in §50, claiming "it is plain that men have agreed to a disproportion-ate and unequal possession of the earth." This attempted defense of economic inequality is not very convincing, relying as it does on the implausible view that, say, a poor person's willingness to use her nation's legal tender amounts to binding consent to accept and respect all of the consequences of a money economy.

p. 40 *are wholly to be put on the account of* labour: This section (with those surrounding it) is often cited as an early statement of "the labor theory of value" (best known from its employment in Marx's economic theory). It is important to see that Locke's is a theory of "use value" and that he distinguishes that from a thing's "natural intrinsic value" (§43).

p. 43 *amongst themselves in distinct parts and parcels of the earth*: Locke appears here to suggest that various international agreements—agreements to give up claims of "natural common right" to land in other nations' possession—have made rightful the "settling" of international boundaries. It is unclear how such "pos-itive agreements" could possibly affect the claims of any persons beyond those who were (either themselves or through their repre-sentatives) actual parties to the agreements in question.

p. 45 *but the perishing of anything uselessly in it*: The conclusion of this section casts into doubt the intended force of the original "enough and as good" proviso. If one's "exceeding the bounds of his just property" has nothing to do with "the largeness of his possession," but only with the "useless perishing" of that possession, it is unclear why leaving "enough and as good" for others to appropriate would necessarily be required.

CHAPTER VI

p. 48 *as if the* mother *had no share in it*: While the target of the chapter is again clearly Filmer, it provides the occasion for one of Locke's few "feminist" moments: Locke for the most part (but not always) manages to remember to substitute "parental power" for the more traditional "paternal power."

p. 50 *are not born in this full state of* equality, *though they are born to it*: The moral status of young children is left somewhat vague by Locke's arguments in this chapter. Young children are not "under" the law of nature, he says, because that law is "promulgated" by reason, the (full) use of which young children lack (§57). But other beings who are not under the law of nature (e.g., wild animals, warmakers) have none of the moral rights that the law of nature defines, leaving us to wonder if young humans are likewise "rightless." Locke vainly attempts to clarify his position by appealing to the civil law's treatment of children (and "incompetents")(§§59–60, 62). The civil law, however, explicitly specifies the legal statuses of such beings, where the law of nature (reason) does not.

p. 50 *but the workmanship of their own maker, the Almighty*: Emphasizing that children are created by God, not by their parents, both undercuts Filmer's arguments for absolute paternal rights over one's children, and also preempts any attempt at a "creationist" interpretation of Chapter V of the *Second Treatise*—i.e., that parents own their children because they labored to produce them.

p. 50 *to whom they were to be accountable for them*: The language of "accountability" here strongly suggests that Locke is thinking of parents as entrusted by God with the care of their (or, more accurately, God's) children, a parental power that can be forfeited by misuse (§65). While Locke famously talks extensively of consent and contracts (or compacts) in this book, the idea of a *trust*—a fiduciary relationship—also figures prominently in his arguments. Most obviously, according to Locke, legitimate governments are not given, but are merely entrusted with, their (forfeitable) powers (§§141–42). Parental powers may be similar, with God as grantor

of the parental trust. I would argue that Locke also takes persons
to be only entrusted (by God) with their own lives. God is the ultimate owner of the persons he creates, but he entrusts each person
with a limited right to manage her own life—a right that, like many
trustees' rights, actually functions like a property right over ourselves in our dealings with other people. This might explain Locke's
occasional "self-ownership" language (e.g., in §§27 and 44).

p. 51 a liberty for every man to do what he lists: This is Filmer's defi-
nition of freedom.

p. 58 *kindness in his education has been more or less*: Locke claims
here (and repeats in §70) that children's duties toward their parents
vary with the degree to which those parents have benefited them—
and can in fact amount to no duty at all, where parents provide no
benefits other than birth (§65). Filial duty thus has for Locke more
the look of a duty of reciprocation for benefits received than it does
a natural duty to "honor" one's biological parents.

p. 62 *what commonwealth they will put themselves under*: Children
must consent in order to inherit land, but this "is no natural tie or
engagement" to "the government of the country"; it is only a condition that commonwealths typically impose, they "not permitting
any part of their dominions to be dismembered" (§117). The child's
consent is still necessary to put her under the authority of a state
or government. Here these claims are used by Locke to show that
paternal power does not include the right to "oblige his posterity to
that government." Locke later repeats these claims (in §116), this
time as part of his more general denial of the position "that being
born under any government, we are naturally subjects to it."

CHAPTER VII

p. 66 *made by a voluntary compact between man and woman*: While
many actual marriages in Locke's day (as in ours) were not genuinely "voluntary" on the part of the woman, remember that Locke
is talking here about what gives partners genuine moral rights
with respect to one another. And genuinely voluntary agreements
do seem an appropriate source of rights between equals, just as
voluntary political agreements do. This view also permits conjugal
rights to vary according to the terms of the marriage contract,
including allowing (once caring for any children is accounted for)
that marriage need not "always be for life" (§81) and that wives
may separate from their husbands where "their contract allows it"
(§82).

p. 69 *the man's share, as the abler and the stronger*: In the midst of his surprisingly liberal claims about conjugal rights, Locke includes here one of his most sexist remarks (about men being "abler and stronger" than women).

p. 70 *absolute dominion and arbitrary power of their masters*: This distinction between servants and "another sort of servants"—i.e., slaves—is critical to Locke's rejection of the morality of chattel slavery (in all cases except those involving enslaved unjust warmakers).

CHAPTER VIII

p. 80 *bound by that consent to be concluded by the* majority: Because he argues that every legitimate society must begin as a "perfect democracy" (§132), governed by majority rule, it might seem that Locke's position could hardly be in starker contrast to Filmer's deeply antidemocratic monarchism. In fact, Locke's (not very convincing) defense of majority rule here is intended as a defense only of the "natural" or "initial" authority of majorities within consensual groups. He allows that groups can (by majority rule) decide that future decision-making will require a super-majority ("any number greater than the majority" [§99]). Presumably, groups could also start by agreeing to be bound in the future by any number of other, nonmajoritarian decision rules. Majority rule is only the initial, default decision rule for morally legitimate incorporated groups. And while civil societies must in this way begin as majority-rule democracies, Locke never suggests that other, nondemocratic forms of government are not also legitimate. Indeed, when Locke discusses "well-framed governments," he mentions "moderated monarchies" (§159)—presumably meaning something very like what he anticipated England's new government would be.

p. 82 *and are not at liberty to begin a new one*: Locke's statement of and response to these two objections certainly stands out in the text. First, of course, he spends a very long time on his responses (§§101–18); but it is interesting to ask why he does so. There is a clear sense in which the second of these two objections has already been answered in the book. And the first objection seems a non sequitur, given that Locke is making a *normative* claim about authority and consent—i.e., that political authority and legitimate subjection require mutual consent—not a *historical* one about how governments actually arose. §104 correctly distinguishes the question "where the right is" from the question "what has been the opinion or practice of mankind." Locke's responses to the objections are at best responses to the second of these questions and seem to be answering his opponents more in their terms than in his own.

p. 84 *under the government and administration of one man*: Locke's long response to this obvious observation about monarchy (lasting though §112) is crucial to his case against Filmer. Locke must distinguish very carefully and clearly, as he does here, between the "naturalness" of *choosing* monarchical rule—of people's naturally choosing to be ruled by their father or by a great warrior—and some people having natural, nonconsensual political authority over others. That some persons are "natural choices" as rulers is perfectly consistent with Locke's claims of natural freedom and equality and of the necessity of consent for legitimate authority (i.e., political power).

p. 90 *But though the* golden age: Locke's reference here to "the golden age" has often been taken to refer to the state of nature ("a state of peace, good will, mutual assistance and preservation" [§19]). But while people living together in a Lockean state of nature can be and has been instantiated in the history of humankind—i.e., whenever people have lived together without having mutually consented to be in one polity together—§§14–15 are straightforwardly inconsistent with identifying the state of nature with any particular (e.g., earlier) historical period.

p. 93 *to a subjection to them and their heirs*: Locke argues at length here (until §118) that the "natural subjection" to political power asserted by his opponents is neither acknowledged by mankind nor claimed by governments themselves. Unfortunately for an argument appealing to "the opinion or practice of mankind," Locke's claims actually seem to support his opponents' view. For he says that "people take no notice" of "the consent of freemen, born under government," concluding "they are naturally subjects as they are men" (§117).

p. 96 *within the territories of that government*: Locke's famous "consent theory" of political obligation, by allowing that tacit consent to government is given by "the very being of anyone within the territories of that government," appears to make consent virtually automatic for any native-born resident (once she reaches the age of consent). While not strictly inconsistent with it, this argument at least sits very uncomfortably with Locke's assertions of our natural freedom from political authority.

p. 97 *under whose jurisdiction it is, as far forth as any subject of it*: Locke here attempts an interesting explanation of how states can acquire permanent and legitimate jurisdiction over a geographical territory (even if the resulting territory may have a "patchwork" quality). If those who consent to create or join a civil society are required as well to submit any land they own to their state's legal jurisdiction, then a state can prevent "dismembering" of this original territory by making it a condition on the sale or inheritance of land that the new owner must consent to the same terms as the old owner did.

p. 98 consent which makes any one a member *of any commonwealth*: Locke attempts here to distinguish between "subjects or members" of a commonwealth and those who merely "submit" to the laws and "live quietly" in that commonwealth. This distinction initially appears to correspond to that (in §119) between express and merely tacit consenters, the former of whom are "perpetually and indispensably obliged" to remain subjects/members, while the latter's obligation of obedience "begins and ends with the enjoyment" (§121). Oddly, however, Locke also appears to say that the "owner" of land in the state "has given nothing but a tacit consent to the government." This would leave the vast majority of propertied citizens in the same group as temporarily "submitting" resident aliens and tourists, reducing the class of "members" to the extremely small group of persons who had taken explicit oaths of allegiance. Presumably, Locke also has in mind (but does not mention) that "members," burdened with their perpetual obligations, enjoy some compensating rights and benefits (perhaps along with the native-born or propertied?) that mere visitors do not.

CHAPTER IX

p. 100 *liberties and estates, which I call by the general name,* property: Here Locke uses "property" in a broader sense than he did in Chapter V. It is property in this broad sense whose preservation is "the great and chief end" of any civil (i.e., consensual) society (§124).

p. 102 Secondly, *the* power of punishing he wholly gives up: The legislative and executive powers of government are here derived from society's "collecting" (and then entrusting to government) those of each member's natural rights that were surrendered in the agreement that created that society. A government's executive powers derive from the surrender to it of each person's "natural executive right" (§§7, 128). Its legislative powers derive from each member surrendering as well whatever aspects of their "natural freedom"

society needs, in order to be able to "preserve" its members
(§§128–29).

CHAPTER X

p. 105 *such is the* form of the commonwealth: There is no "natural"
form of legitimate government. The members of a civil society may
choose to structure their government "as they think good."

p. 105 *I consent with him to change it for a better*: It is important that
Locke be very clear about what he means by "commonwealth,"
given the connotations of that term after the execution of Charles I
(when "commonwealth" replaced "kingdom" in England's official
name). Also, Locke's use of *"king James the first"* (here and in
§200) is probably the best evidence that at least part of the *Second
Treatise* was written before James II became king—since the corresponding passages in the first edition of the *Second Treatise* read
simply "K. James himself" and "King James" (as if there were only
one king by that name).

CHAPTER XI

p. 108 *an eternal rule to all men,* legislators *as well as others*: In
§§135–37 Locke uses both logical and prudential arguments for
the limited nature of governmental powers. That the law of nature
is "an eternal rule" both limits our natural freedom and, consequently, logically limits the ways in which we can empower governments. But Locke also argues in §137 that it would be
prudentially irrational to give a government absolute power. The
suggestion that it "cannot be supposed that they should intend" to
grant absolute power is also perhaps meant to argue that any tacit
(or otherwise inexplicit) entrusting of power by the people cannot
reasonably be interpreted to include empowering government to
act arbitrarily, since it would be unconscionably stupid for the
people to do so (see also §§93, 131, 164).

p. 111 *any part of his* property *without his own consent*: This passage
is sometimes taken to refer to taxation and to require for it a second level of personal consent. That would be puzzling, given that
the power to tax is surely one of those necessary rights that the
(majority of the) people must entrust to their government. This
passage seems best read as a prohibition not on taxation without
personal consent, but simply on the arbitrary seizure of property
by government. §140 more obviously concerns taxes, which it is
"fit" that everyone should pay; and there Locke appears only to

insist that taxation be consented to by the majority "or their representatives" (rather than being levied by officials on their "own authority").

p. 112 absolute power, *where it is necessary, is* not arbitrary *by being absolute*: Locke mostly seems to use "arbitrary" and "absolute" interchangeably, both meaning "unlimited." In this one passage, however, he attempts to distinguish the two terms. Unfortunately, the example he gives to clarify the distinction (of a "superior officer's" right to "absolute obedience") is inadequate to do so. I suspect Locke is here thinking of "absolute" power as being unlimited, but only within or with respect to a particular sphere or range of actions, while "arbitrary" power is both unlimited and reaches every possible sphere. Unfortunately, he elsewhere uses these terms in other ways, as when (in §210) he characterizes justified prerogative as an "arbitrary power."

CHAPTER XII

p. 116 *to take care that they make them for the public good*: Locke argues here for the separation of legislative and executive powers. It is unclear whether he intends to claim only that it is wise to separate them—that "well-ordered commonwealths" or "well-framed governments" (§159) will do this—or, more strongly, that failure to separate these powers would de-legitimize an otherwise civil society.

p. 116 *and may be called* federative: This third power of government, Locke explains (in §145), is the power to deal with those who are not part of the society—that is, those with respect to whom the society's members remain in the state of nature. Individuals' natural rights (to transact with and judge the conduct of all other persons), once they are in part conveyed to society and entrusted to government, can be divided into the government's right to deal with those who are now members—its legislative and executive powers—and its right to deal with those who remain nonmembers—its federative power.

CHAPTER XIII

p. 122 *when the original constitution or the public exigencies require it*: The position taken here (and in §§156 and 167) is clearly intended to indict Charles II, who repeatedly attempted to prevent Parliament from meeting. Locke characterizes such acts as initiating "a state of war with the people," thus justifying forceful resistance to and punishment of the king.

p. 124 *numerous in people and powerful in riches*: An important part of Shaftesbury's political agenda was the elimination of "rotten boroughs"—towns entitled to representation, but having a very small electorate that was typically manipulated by a rich land-owner. Locke argues here that in representative governments, people have a right to fair, proportionate representation and the elimination of corrupt representation that relies on "the bare name of a town."

CHAPTER XIV

p. 128 *where it can prove no prejudice to the innocent*: In light of Locke's obvious concerns about abuses of the executive power, it is perhaps surprising to see in this chapter the extent to which Locke is willing to allow executive prerogative to operate. Prerogative is characterized here as executive discretion to act for the good of society—"the power of doing public good without a rule" (§166)—when (e.g.) existing law gives no clear guidance, when rapid response to a crisis is required, or when the law is too severe in a particular case and a pardon is appropriate.

p. 132 *they have no judge on earth, but to* appeal to heaven: The "appeal to heaven" (initially introduced in §§20–21) refers to resorting to force (when one judges it necessary) because of the absence of a neutral judge on earth to hear one's appeal. That Locke thinks "any single man" has the right to do this—i.e., to use force against a king or government that wrongs him—is an extraordinarily strong version of a right of political resistance.

CHAPTER XV

p. 134 *it may not, perhaps, be amiss to consider them here together*: This entire chapter is simply a summary of the preceding arguments concerning differences between the different kinds of powers (rights, authority) Locke has discussed.

CHAPTER XVI

p. 138 *reckon conquest as one of the originals of government*: Locke almost certainly has in mind Grotius and Hobbes, among the "many" who have made this mistake.

p. 142 *have lived upon fair terms with him*: This is an interesting logical point about the guilt of the general citizenry of a nation that makes unjust war on others. Because people themselves lack the right to make unjust war, Locke argues, they lack the power to authorize their government to make unjust war on their behalf. The people, then, even if they appear to have tried to authorize the unjust war, cannot be held complicit in such a war unless "they actually abet it."

p. 144 *but gave me no title to his goods*: Locke's use here of the analogy of the would-be thief—who may be killed (or enslaved) as a warmaker, but who may not be robbed and released—is confusing. Locke plainly says (here and elsewhere) that any unjust use of force—such as the thief's—initiates a state of war and forfeits the aggressor's life. But he also says that unjust warmakers have, by their actions, "lost their estates" (§85)—that is, they have lost any claim to their material property. So robbing the would-be thief could not be a wrong to him. And it is unclear who would have a better claim to the thief's now-unowned money than his intended victim.

p. 145 *preferable title of those who are in danger to perish without it*: This may be the only place where Locke directly discusses the possibility of a conflict of rights—in this case, the conflict between a just conqueror's right to reparation from the conquered and the right of the warmaker's wife and children to his property. In this case, Locke says that the latter claim, being the more "pressing and preferable title," should prevail.

p. 148 *to inherit with his brethren his father's goods*: It is at least surprising to find the right to inherit elevated to the same standing as the right to natural freedom. Locke may have wished to emphasize this right in response to then-current political uses of the English legal practice of making convicted felons—including those convicted of "political" crimes—forfeit all property.

CHAPTER XVIII

p. 154 exercise of power beyond right, *which nobody can have a right to*: Locke plainly intends here not that just any "exercise of power beyond right"—including, say, my beating you with a stick—constitutes "tyranny." Rather, he means that tyranny is the exercise of specifically *political* power beyond right.

p. 161 *religion underhand favoured . . . which is readiest to introduce it*: "Religion underhand favoured" most likely refers to the actions of Charles II in support of Catholicism. The use in this section of "*a long train of actions*" anticipates the far more famous "long train of abuses" passage in §225, the wording of which clearly later influenced Jefferson's in the American Declaration of Independence.

CHAPTER XIX

p. 162 *and act as one body, and so be distinct commonwealth*: Locke's distinction between the dissolution of society and the dissolution of government is important to his understanding of what resistance to or rebellion against the crown would bring about. Despite the removal of the king, the English people, bound together as a consensual society, would still continue as one body—with each member bound by the majority's decisions concerning instituting a new government. Return to a state of nature (or state of war) with respect to one another would not be the result of such a revolution (supposing only, as Locke appears to be, that England constituted a civil society in the first place).

p. 164 *Such a form of government supposed, it is evident*: Locke here describes the specific form of government that he understands England to have, in order to list in that context the particular abuses of which Charles and James were guilty. Charles both "changed" and "hindered" the assembly of the legislative (§§214–15); both Charles and James altered the electoral process (§216) and attempted to deliver "the people into the subjection of a foreign power" (i.e., the Pope in Rome and the Catholic king of France). James was also accused of having "abandoned his charge" (§219) by fleeing England.

p. 170 *uncertain humour of the people is to expose it to certain ruin*: Locke here begins a long defense (lasting until §230) against the charge that his theory of justified resistance will lead to constant and chaotic changes of government or revolutions. His replies are, first, that theories really don't matter much in such affairs: regardless of what theories are propounded, the people will inevitably change things whenever they are "*generally ill-treated*" (§224). Second, the people are naturally slow to change things without (in his now-famous phrase) "a long train of abuses, prevarications and artifices, all tending the same way" (§§225). Indeed, Locke further claims that, if theory matters at all to practice, his theory is the "*best fence against rebellion*" (§226), since it will show those who are "truly and properly *rebels*"—governments acting contrary to their trust—"the danger and injustice" of their conduct.

p. 182 *Barclay, and those of his opinion, would do well to tell us*: The idea that a king can "dethrone himself" by breach of trust, of course, permits the dethroned king to be treated like "any other man" who makes unjust war on others. Traditional concerns about the sacredness of the king's person are thus side-stepped, since "he is no king."

p. 184 *have still a power to discard him when he fails in his trust*: God is the ultimate judge of right and wrong; but on earth, "every man is judge for himself" in private cases of war, and "the people shall be judge" in matters of the powers entrusted to government. Locke writes as if this last point is a simple function of the nature of any fiduciary relationship. He probably means to say that this is at least true where there is no earthly court empowered to judge disagreements between grantors and their trustees—in this case, between the people and their government.

ABOUT THE NORTON LIBRARY

Exciting texts you can't get anywhere else

The Norton Library is the only series that offers an inexpensive, student-friendly edition of Emily Wilson's groundbreaking version of Homer's *Odyssey*, or Carole Satyamurti's thrilling, prize-winning rendition of the *Mahabharata*, or Michael Palma's virtuoso *terza rima* translation of Dante's *Inferno*—to name just three of its unique offerings. Distinctive translations like these, exclusive to the Norton Library, are the cornerstone of the list, but even texts originally written in English offer unique distinctions. Where else, for instance, will you find an edition of John Stuart Mill's *Utilitarianism* edited and introduced by Peter Singer? Only in the Norton Library.

The Norton touch

For more than 75 years, W. W. Norton has published texts that are edited with the needs of students in mind. Volumes in the Norton Library all offer editorial features that help students read with more understanding and pleasure—to encounter the world of the work on its own terms, but also to have a trusted travel guide navigate them through that world's unfamiliar territory.

Easy to afford, a pleasure to own

Volumes in the Norton Library are inexpensive—among the most affordable texts available—but they are designed and produced with great care to be easy on the eyes, comfortable in the hand, and a pleasure to read and re-read over a lifetime.

W. W. NORTON & COMPANY
Independent Publishers Since 1923